Desert Voices
The Edge Effect

Desert Voices
The Edge Effect
Tessa Bielecki and David Denny

Sand & Sky
Publishing

Sand and Sky Publishing is an imprint of the Desert Foundation, an informal circle of friends exploring the wisdom of the world's deserts with a special focus on peace and reconciliation between the three Abrahamic traditions that grow out of the desert: Judaism, Christianity, and Islam. Proceeds from the sale of this book support the Desert Foundation, a 501 (c)(3) organization founded in June 2005 by Tessa Bielecki and David Denny. Contributions are tax-deductible.

Sand and Sky Publishing
P.O. Box 1000
Crestone, CO 81131

www.sandandsky.org
sandandsky@desertfound.org
Available at www.CreateSpace.com/5660709

Book design and composition by Tessa Bielecki
Cover design and computer graphics by David Denny
Cover artwork by Marilyn L. Denny

Manufactured in the United States of America
ISBN-13: 978-0692507698 (Sand and Sky Publishing)
ISBN-10: 0692507698

For
Dennis, Kiki, Laura, Netanel, Paul, Pegge, and Dorie,
who encourage our desert voices

Contents

Part 1: Desert Love Affair

Life nowhere appears so brave, so bright, so full of oracle and miracle as in the desert.
Edward Abbey

Part 2: The Tent of Meeting

*If I do not discover in myself the terrain where the Hindu,
the Muslim, the Jew and the atheist may have a place—in my
heart, in my intelligence, in my life —I will never be able to
enter into a genuine dialogue.*
Raimon Panikkar

Part 3: Walls and Bridges

*Jerusalem, Jerusalem, you who kill the prophets and stone
those sent to you, how many times I yearned to gather your
children together, as a hen gathers her young under her wings,
but you were unwilling.*
Matthew 23:37

Part 4: The Inner Desert

The inner desert arises primarily from grief: the universal desert of unchosen loss and death, pain that grinds the soul to dust and bears within it the threat of despair as well as hope for transformation and compassion.
David Denny

Introduction: Desert Harvest

David Denny and Tessa Bielecki

Native American corn grows in the desert without irrigation. Hopi corn, or maize, may be planted as deep as eighteen inches, where the earth harbors just enough moisture to trigger germination. These seeds have enough energy to travel a long way to sunlight. The plants are short and far apart. But the yield is nutritious.

Desert Voices is similar. It gathers the harvest of the Desert Foundation's first decade of writing. At the end of every year, we both think, "We haven't done much." We live a simple wilderness life under a vast sky, near towering mountains that tend to dwarf all human activity. We see more deer than people. But then we look back and are surprised by the meaning in our lives, by how far the seeds we plant travel and bear nutritious food for thought and prayer and contemplative action in the world.

Desert Love Affair

Our harvest here in *Desert Voices* appears in four parts. In Part One, "Desert Love Affair," we reflect on our falling in love with the geographical desert and on the experience of the earliest monks, known as the "Desert Fathers and Mothers."

The desert traditionally fosters a spirit of hospitality and dialogue with the "stranger." In our own experience, the "desert" life includes dedication to humble interspiritual dialogue and simple sustainable living. We hope you will find encouraging, timeless wisdom in these twenty-first century reflections. We believe that silence, simplicity, and solitude are not obsolete in a digital world of speed, sound bites, and social media. We hope you will agree.

Tent of Meeting

Part Two, "Tent of Meeting," takes its title from the Hebrew Testament's description of the portable desert sanctuary the Jews erected during their flight from slavery in Egypt in search of the Promised Land. Beneath that canopy, the Jewish people encountered Yahweh on their way through the desert. We interpret the Tent here as a sacred "place" where the descendants of Abraham and Sarah may meet one another and the One in whose image we are created, the One with whom Jews, Christians, and Muslims have all made sacred covenants.

Spiritual growth involves humble listening to the "stranger." If religion strays into ideology, it provokes violent resistance to "contamination" from the "other." But if our tradition nurtures a transformative, divinizing humility, then contact with the "other" is not contamination but *cross-fertilization*. Contact may make each community healthier and wiser and allow each to embody its unique identity and promise.

The Edge Effect: Walls and Bridges

"Ecotone" is an ecological term which describes an area where two communities overlap, as in marshes where land and water meet, estuaries where salt and fresh water mingle, or areas where trees give way to grasslands. An ecotone creates an "edge effect," where life flourishes. Some species find these places ideal for courtship, foraging for food, or nesting.

This leads us to Part Three of *Desert Voices*, "Walls and Bridges," perhaps the most discouraging and yet hopeful part of our reflections. It includes our grappling with the notion of *"political holiness"* in the context of heartbreaking conflicts between Jews, Christians, and Muslims in Israel/Palestine.

Some spiritual traditions have divided the sacred and the profane, the spiritual and the mundane, heaven and earth, prayer and politics. We are Christians, and we believe that the Incarnation of Jesus in the flesh has broken down these splits.

The "edge effect" may allow us to hope that a wall of separation and conflict may be transfigured into a fertile ecotone providing food, shelter, and—who knows?—maybe even courtship. We admit that it is cheeky, even absurd, to encourage peace between Jews, Christians, and Muslims in the Holy Land when we Christians suffer chasms of mistrust and suspicion within our own flock. But this is our vocation, and we're sticking with it.

The Inner Desert

Part Four, "The Inner Desert," arises from the universal human experience of grief: the desert of unchosen loss, death, and exposure to pain that grinds the soul to dust and bears within it the threat of despair as well as the hope of transformation, compassion, and mercy. Abraham and Sarah, Jesus, Muhammad and countless saints from each of the Abrahamic traditions discovered the desert as a harsh school of human, moral, and spiritual maturation.

So if you have little interest in the geographical desert or feel overwhelmed by the difficulties of interspiritual dialogue and the search for justice in the Holy Land, you may wish to begin by reading this final section of *Desert Voices*. No one evades this inner desert. If we learn to embrace it, we may discover it as a land of manna or maize and a birthplace for freedom.

Desert Writing for the World

Some years ago, a friend wrote that our writing vocation "demonstrates... that a call to the desert is also a call to the world, that an earnest seeking after God in silence and emptiness is the natural corollary to a profound, intimate love of the created order, and that the beautiful work of human hands is not an impediment to the soul's stillness but a pathway to it."

We hope that we live up to this vision through thoughtful writing that may not only encourage contemplation, but compassionate action in the quest for justice and peace.

Part 1
Desert Love Affair

Life nowhere appears so brave, so bright, so full of
oracle and miracle as in the desert.

Edward Abbey

1
Sounding the Silence

What We Hear in the Desert

Tessa Bielecki Interviews David Denny

Tessa: Why focus on the desert?

David: In a world of mobility and displacement, many long to recover the importance of the sense of place in general. A common Arabic greeting is *"Ahlan wa sahlan,"* which roughly translates, "These are your people and this is your land." So our Desert Foundation is an informal circle of friends who share a love for the desert: the land, the people and the spirituality.

T: What if you don't live in the physical desert?

D: The desert is not only geography, but spirit. Some desert places, such as the American Southwest and the Middle East, are considered sacred and have also become "a battleground of conflicting claims based on a multitude of cultural voices," as Belden Lane wrote in *Landscapes of the Sacred.* I hope we will shed light on such claims and highlight peaceful solutions to these geo-spiritual conflicts.

T: **At this sorrowful moment in history when the sons and daughters of Abraham are shedding each other's blood throughout the world, we emphasize peace between Jews, Christians, and Muslims.**

D: Yes. Peacemaking happens best when we develop a way of life that includes an understanding of desert spirituality. That is, in addition to being geography and spirit, the desert, as I'm fond of saying, has traditionally fostered hospitality, respect, and dialogue with the stranger. This spirit arises from various aspects of the "desert": a freely chosen dedication to humility, interfaith dialogue, and simple, ecologically sustainable living.

T: **What do you mean by "sustainable living"?**

D: You and I live simple hermit lives dedicated to prayer, study, writing, and manual labor: "chop wood, carry water." I believe that what we have to give to others depends on the mysterious solitary life to which Christ calls us. Some folks study the desert and its peoples as a science. Some religious consider the desert a metaphor. But for us it's a tangible place as well as the metaphorical birthplace of wisdom that's meant to be shared. It's where we live—physically, metaphysically, and simply.

T: **What about the "inner desert"?**

D: As I mentioned in "Desert Harvest," the inner desert arises primarily from grief, a universal human experience: the desert of unchosen loss, death, of exposure to pain that grinds the soul to dust and bears within it the threat of despair as well as the hope of transformation, compassion, and a life dedicated to justice and mercy.

T: **Is the inner desert a dark night of the soul?**

D: Mystics such as St. John of the Cross also acknowledge another dimension of the inner desert: a loss of the faith that sustained us at an earlier time in our lives. Beloved images of

God may no longer speak to us. Ways of praying or meditating may feel utterly fruitless. Old certainties feel embarrassingly inadequate. How could we have been so smug? John said that as faith gets deeper, it gets darker. This can be deeply disturbing, but it is not the loss of faith; it is the maturation of faith. John called it a guiding night, a night more beautiful than the dawn because it unites the lover with the beloved.

T: Can you speak more out of your own personal experience?

D: My mother, Marilyn Denny, suffered from Alzheimer's disease for almost eight years and finally died from a terrible fall. Her brain could no longer tell her how to put one foot in front of another and walk. The pain of watching my mother struggle, and my father with her, truly ground my soul to dust. It sometimes led me to the brink of despair. Mom's hospice chaplain told me that he was with her one day when she was extremely agitated and cried out, "My God, my God!" He expected her to continue with the words of Psalm 22, the last words of Jesus in the Gospels of Matthew and Mark: "Why have you forsaken me?" Instead, she relaxed and uttered, "Thank you!" Those may have been her last words. Of course I wish I could have been there. Why would she say that in the presence of someone who is practically a stranger? That, too, is part of the desert experience: hearing a word of hope secondhand, and trusting.

T: Many of us think of the desert as a wasteland.

D: For many people, the desert is a place to avoid, a place of banishment or grief, or simply useless and vacant. In English, when we say that a place is "deserted," we usually mean that we find nothing significant there. But the Arabic verb *ashara* means to enter the desert willingly, for there, according to *The Sacred Desert* by David Jaspers, "If one knows where to look, there are springs and wells of water and places of life." That's why Isaiah 35:1 so aptly describes the heart of the universal desert experience: *The desert and the dry land will be glad; the wilderness will rejoice and blossom.*

T: **I love camels so much as a symbol of the desert, my hermitage is full of camel art in many forms. So I'm glad we use them as the logo for our** *Caravans* **newsletter.**

D: The word "caravan" comes from the Italian *caravana,* from the Persian *karwaan*: a company of travelers on a journey through desert regions. So our own *Caravans* unites a wide and diverse company of travelers, a circle of friends, who venture together through both inner and outer desert landscapes.

You do not have to experience the geographical desert. Whether you live in San Francisco or the Sahara, Moscow or the Mohave, Saigon or the Sonoran, the call of the desert is the same. God speaks to the intimate depths of every human heart through the prophet Hosea: "I will lead you into the desert, and there I will speak to your heart" (Hosea 2:14).

Tessa Bielecki

5

2
Homeland of My Heart

Falling in Love with the Desert

Tessa Bielecki

I grew up in New England, a countryside of lush green hills, singing streams, and verdant forests of oak and maple. In springtime I picked bouquets of wildflowers and in summer romped through the tall grasses full of daisies. When the trees turned crimson and gold in autumn, I gathered bundles of leaves and pressed them between the pages of my beloved books. In winter I built bonfires, skated on the ponds and went tobogganing down the steep hills.

Matter Matters

Instinctually I knew that "matter matters." Later I came to understand more theologically that "The Word became flesh and dwelt among us" (John 1:14), that is, that God permeates all the matter of the universe. I prayed with my favorite saint, Teresa of Avila, "Oh Lord, you are on the earth and clothed with it."

In college I discovered the twentieth-century mystic-scientist, Pierre de Teilhard de Chardin, who made my heart soar when he wrote about "the spiritual power of matter" and sang rhapsodically, "Matter,...I surrender myself to your mighty layers,...The virtue of Christ has passed into you."

I met William McNamara in college, too, and he taught me not only about the Carmelite monastic tradition but about "the desert experience." I really learned what he meant as the years of my life unfolded. He said, "The desert experience is a long, arduous trek through purgation into Paradise. It begins with a free decision to suffer and ends with the uproariously happy surprise of being in harmony with the universe and in love with all that is."

I first saw the vast magnificent desert of the American Southwest in 1966 and have lived there since 1967. It was love at first sight, the most dramatic epiphany of my life. It felt like coming home—to myself. I recognized the outer landscape as a mirror of my inner soulscape.

The desert is the homeland of my heart. I don't find it barren as many do. I find the desert spacious, a perfect embodiment of what my Buddhist friends mean by *sunyata*, infinite spaciousness. My spiritual path is cultivating a heart as spacious as the desert: wide open to every direction of the compass, wide open to every creature that walks, flies, or crawls through it, wide open to every change in the weather: darkness and light, sun and rain, aridity and dew, heat, cold, and wind.

St. Teresa, who grew to become my best friend, called the human soul an interior castle. "Let's not imagine that we are hollow inside," she wrote. "The soul is capable of much more than we can imagine." This infinite and noble spaciousness is what I learn from the desert.

3

Desert Tales and Disciplines

Sink or Swim?

David Denny

When I first listened to Henri Nouwen's talks on desert spirituality, they reminded me of Basque philosopher Miguel de Unamuno's contention that the best way to move into the future is backwards. That is, instead of running toward a future that may be a rootless fantasy, we do well to look back in time to glean fruits we may have rejected along our pilgrim way.

Nouwen, the late Dutch Roman Catholic priest who helped spiritual leaders recapture their vocations as "wounded healers," plumbed the wisdom of the Egyptian Desert Fathers and Mothers of the fourth and fifth centuries. He describes a malaise that afflicts many of us.

Heart Stories

In a "mind-minded" world, our religious lives are often driven by study and talk about God and the problems of life. But talk and thinking will not lead us through the fire of transformation to still waters. So Nouwen looks not to the thought, but to the disciplines and stories of the Desert Fathers and Mothers who addressed the heart, the whole person, rather than the mind alone.

Nouwen ponders three fundamental desert counsels: flee, be silent, and pray always. Our activist, extroverted, earth- and body-affirming attitudes may tempt us to translate these commands as escape, stifle your voice, and settle into self-righteous pietism. But Nouwen deftly helps us acknowledge the anger and greed that lurk within us. With a soft touch, he allows us to admit that before we can "improve," we must die to our compulsive need for affirmation from outside ourselves.

The desert monks' flight, silence, and prayer, Nouwen insists, were a mature response to a human condition that is basically a "shipwreck," as Thomas Merton put it. Is it selfish to swim for help instead of drowning in a kind of "solidarity" with our fellow victims?

This "swim" is a purifying pilgrimage into the humbling revelation of our human brokenness and a transforming encounter with forgiveness. It is an escape from a painful situation in order to move from fruitless suffering to fruitful, humanizing and healing suffering: the birth pangs of radical compassion.

If we make our way into this silent wilderness, Nouwen claims, we touch the mystery of the future, the kingdom of heaven, and we may return to the present world's problems, tragedies and hopelessness without feeling or being impotent and overwhelmed. By the grace of God, we may grow through the discipline of simple daily prayer into a habit of deep listening to the Spirit. We may learn to speak, out of silence, awe, wonder and wisdom, words that differ from the wordiness of advertising and propaganda.

As Nouwen puts it, much may be said while little is spoken. What we say after we have been broken and revivified in the desert will not draw attention toward us but toward the Mystery dwelling within and beyond. Such words transmit creative and recreative power.

4
The Wisdom of the Desert

Challenging a Shipwrecked Society

Tessa Bielecki

The Wisdom of the Desert was one of Thomas Merton's favorites among his own books, probably because he wanted to spend his last years as a hermit at the Trappist Monastery of Gethsemane. Merton did his own translation of the sayings and parables of the fourth-century Christian "Fathers and Mothers of the Desert" who sought a life of solitude and contemplation in the deserts of Egypt, Palestine, Arabia, and Persia.

What happened in the fourth century? Paradoxically, the Roman Emperor Constantine became Christian and made Christianity the official religion of the Roman Empire. The first hermits found this "decadent" and did not accept the cross as a sign of temporal power, as the Emperor did.

Shipwrecked Society

For years I've been fascinated by the way Merton described "worldly" society as a "shipwreck." He claimed that each of us needs to make "a clean break with a conventional, accepted social context in order to swim for one's life." This isn't selfish, he insists.

The first hermits "who left the world as though escaping from a wreck, did not merely intend to save themselves. They knew that they were helpless to do any good for others as long as they floundered about in the wreckage. But once they got a foothold on solid ground, things were different. Then they had not only the power but even the obligation to pull the whole world to safety after them." Merton continued in the same vein:

> *[The Fathers and Mothers of the Desert] did not believe in letting themselves be passively guided and ruled by a decadent state, and believed that there was a way of getting along without slavish dependence on*

accepted, conventional values....What [they] sought most of all was their own true self, in Christ. And in order to do this, they had to reject the false, formal self, fabricated under social compulsion in "the world." They sought a way to God that was uncharted and freely chosen, not inherited from others who had mapped it out beforehand. They sought a God whom they alone could find, not one who was "given" in a set, stereotyped form by somebody else.... There was nothing to which they had to "conform" except the secret, hidden, inscrutable will of God which might differ very notably from one [person] to another.

Challenging Questions

I've been challenged by this for decades and keep asking myself these questions.

Is my society shipwrecked? Am I floundering?

How do I need to swim for my life?

Do I live in a decadent society?

How am I passively guided by it?

How do I depend on accepted conventional values?

Am I prepared to seek my own true self, in Christ?

And to reject my false self?

What does my false self look like?

What social compulsions have fabricated it?

What does my true self look like?

What do I need to do to realize it?

Have I freely chosen my way to God?

Did I inherit it from others who mapped it out beforehand?

Is there an appropriate balance between the two?

How much do I conform?

Am I courageous enough to be different?

To follow the inscrutable will of God for me?

The Humility of Abba Moses

I've read Merton's little book again and again over the years, and my favorite story is always Number XLI (41).

A brother in Scete happened to commit a fault, and the elders assembled, and sent for Abba Moses to join them. He, however, did not want to come. The priest sent him a message, saying: Come, the community of the brethren is waiting for you. So he arose and started off. And taking with him a very old basket full of holes, he filled it with sand, and carried it behind him. The elders came out to meet him, and said: What is this, Father? [Abba Moses] replied: My sins are running out behind me, and I do not see them, and today I come to judge the sins of another. They, hearing this, said nothing to the brother but pardoned him.

5
Fierce and Sacred Landscapes

Exploring Desert and Mountain Spirituality

Tessa Bielecki Meets Belden Lane

Dr. Belden C. Lane is an avid storyteller and backpacker whose books include The Solace of Fierce Landscapes: Exploring Desert and Mountain Spirituality *and* Landscapes of the Sacred: Narrative and Geography in American Spirituality. *Now retired, Lane was a Professor of Theological Studies at St. Louis University, a Presbyterian minister teaching the history of spirituality on a Jesuit faculty. When Tessa Bielecki attended his talks in Denver, he called himself a "recovering scholar" who wants to write with fewer footnotes. Here is what Tessa learned from Dr. Lane.*

Why are we so attracted to wild places?

We love wilderness because it nurtures something in us. The vertical edge of the mountain and the horizontal edge of the desert take us to the edge of ourselves. The wilderness is both fascinating and terrifying, a place of death and a promise of new life. The Spaniards called Death Valley "the palm of God's hand" because it was both a place to die and a place of intimacy with God.

Why do we call desert spirituality "God's call to life on the margins"?

Psychologist James Hillman says we are torn between peak and valley experiences. We experience the dark depths of the vale and "liminal" places where the "normal" in our lives breaks down. Mark gives us a desert Gospel. Matthew tells us five different mountain stories. Jesus leads us across boundaries and out to the edges.

How can we be positive about the "seeming indifference" of the wilderness?

How did the wild canyon cliff change when your world fell apart? It remained constant in its immensity and majesty. The vast emptiness of the wilderness invites us to let go. It teaches us not to take ourselves so seriously. What the Desert Fathers called *apatheia* is an indifference to unimportant things. In our twisted, militaristic, consumer society, where we're so preoccupied with our own reputations, what do we need to ignore and what do we need to love? When we let go of what needs to die in us, we set free what needs to be born in us. So we need a *selective* practice of indifference aimed at the false self in order to affirm the true self.

What qualities should we admire in the Desert Monks?

The Desert Fathers and Mothers practiced forgiveness and would not judge others or make themselves look better by making others look worse. The older monks were really sensitive to the younger and weaker monks, usually giving them the benefit of the doubt. They focused on the best in everyone and insisted that our failures are sources of our transformation. What we do not transform in ourselves, we transmit to others. Abba Poemon said that our woundedness first festers in the heart, then shows up on our faces, then comes out in our words, and then in our deeds. We end up doing to others what was done to us. We need to embrace our woundedness and work with it.

What do we mean when we say "the gift is in the wound"? How do we grow through pain?

The broken places where we have been hurt in our lives are the points where God is most able to touch and heal us. Our wounds and mistakes are sources of grace. When we're wounded, we usually cope initially through denial and defenses to protect ourselves from more pain. We pretend we're "in control" and project a strong, impregnable *persona*. We suppress our own feelings and needs and take care of others as an escape. But eventually the wound erupts again, we lose our defenses, and the props are knocked out from under us. We experience trauma and a real kind of death.

We finally learn to share our vulnerability and live out of the wound instead of hiding it. Leonard Cohen's song "Anthem" beautifully expresses the new life we finally come to: "Ring the bells that still can ring / Forget your perfect offering / There is a crack, a crack in everything / That's how the light gets in." This is the pattern of desert spirituality: woundedness, defense and denial, trauma and death, and finally brand new life.

How do we grow through our fear?

How do we face anything that frightens us? We can run away from it, or we can look squarely at it. If we face our fear and name it, it's not as terrifying. We need to follow our fear until we recognize what has to die in us, and then let it go. What threatens to kill us can then become a profound source of hope and healing.

What makes a space sacred to us?

The places that are truly sacred to us are often ordinary places where something extraordinary happens. The places that feed us, where we go to be put back together again, mediate the sacred to us. They carry energy, power, and immediacy and invite us to be present.

But does simply moving into an allegedly sacred place automatically make us present to it?

No, we may need "rituals of entry." Silence helps. Moving slowly helps, too. We need to explore a place to see what's growing there, engage all our senses, maybe pick up a rock and hold it in our hands. Kentucky farmer and poet Wendell Berry says that we can't truly change "places" as easily as we can transport our bodies. The faster we go, the longer it takes to bring our minds to a stop. So he encourages us to move through a landscape as if we were one of its details.

6
Imprint of the Desert

Wilfred Thesiger's *Arabian Sands*

David Denny

*A*rabian Sands by Wilfred Thesiger recounts the young man's explorations in the southern Arabian Peninsula in the 1940s, just before the great oil companies arrived to create an international energy hub and destroy the pre-petroleum-age Bedouin culture.

If you are thirsty for descriptions of the sheer physical atmosphere of the desert and portraits of men who adapted to its rigors and inherited an ancient Bedouin tradition, this book will satisfy your thirst. It teems with paradoxes, including descriptions of fierce loyalty and hospitality and customs that to us seem terrifyingly primal, such as circumcision rites for teenage boys. But Thesiger's portraits of bin Kabina and bin Ghabaisha, two young Bedouin friends, are touching and revealing.

Thesiger himself was a strange combination: an upper class Englishman who had connections that enabled him to travel in remote areas, and who suffered an "aching nostalgia for this comfortless yet satisfying life" in the desert. He mapped uncharted regions, knowing that "the maps [he] made helped others, with more material aims, to visit and corrupt a people whose spirit once lit the desert like a flame."

Desert and River Islam

Thesiger's descriptions of village versus desert life challenge the notion put forth by Gaber Asfour, an Egyptian writer who distinguishes between "desert" and "river" Islam. According to Asfour, al-Qaeda founder Osama bin Laden represented "the intolerant 'trend of transmission' associated with the harsh desert," whereas the cosmopolitan culture of life along the Nile represents a more tolerant "Islam of the rivers."

In the town of Laila, Thesiger had a terrible time getting supplies for one of his journeys. His Bedouin fellows "were cursed and spat at for bringing an infidel into the town." Shopkeepers said they would accept the infidel's money only if it were publicly washed! The Bedouins were scandalized. "They say you are an infidel," raged bin Kabina, "but you are a hundred times better than such Muslims as these." So in this case at least, the desert was not the birthplace of fanaticism, but a hospitable willingness to judge a man on his merits, not his religion.

How about the Bedouins' attitude toward Jews? At the palace of Shakhbut, ruler of Abu Dhabi, Thesiger hears the sheikh's account of the war in Palestine, soon to become Israel. Shakhbut ends with a diatribe against the Jews, and a puzzled bin Kabina leans over to Thesiger, whispering, "Who are the Jews? Are they Arabs?" Fifty years later, it is hard to imagine a Bedouin who has never heard of Jews or the state of Israel.

Arabian Sands includes countless beautifully written passages. Thesiger's description of Zayid bin Sultan and a hawking expedition with this Bedouin prince seems to come from the Middle Ages rather than from the 1940s.

T.E. Lawrence wrote, "Bedouin ways were hard, even for those brought up in them and for strangers terrible: a death in life." No man can live this life and emerge unchanged. He will carry, however faint, the imprint of the desert, the brand which marks the nomad; and he will have within him the yearning to return, weak or insistent according to his nature. For this cruel land can cast a spell which no temperate clime can match.

7

Living in a Desert Hogan

A Flowering Solitude

Tessa Bielecki

I'm sitting at the big picture window at the Hogan, looking over rabbit brush, piñon pine and golden rice grass to the San Juan Mountains, across the open valley to the west. The blazing sunset has just subsided, and I await the appearance of Venus, Jupiter and Saturn in a rare alignment of planets that will not recur for many years. The lone female coyote who frequents this area now just passed by, along her usual evening route. The loud howling of the larger pack, close to my house, has kept me awake at night.

Sangre de Cristo

In the east, Sirius, the Dog Star, trails Orion the Hunter over the Sangre de Cristo Mountains. "See how red the mountains are growing," says a young man at sunset to Archbishop Jean Latour in *Death Comes for the Archbishop,* the superb novel by Willa Cather, which I have just read for the umpteenth time. The archbishop replies: "Yes, Sangre de Cristo; but no matter how scarlet the sunset... [the mountains never become] the color of living blood, but the color of the dried blood of saints and martyrs preserved in old churches in Rome."

The Sky, the Sky!

Through Cather's poetic language, Latour also reflects on the beauty of the southwestern sky which has swept me away these days: "The sky was as full of motion and change as the desert beneath it was monotonous and still,—and there was so much sky, more than at sea, more than anywhere else in the world; Elsewhere the sky is the roof of the world; but here the earth was the floor of the sky. The landscape one longed for when one was far away...was the sky, the sky!"

Latour was the first bishop of New Mexico, a vast territory that eventually included all of Arizona and then the even wilder country of Colorado. (In "real life" his name was Jean Baptiste Lamy.) At one point this dedicated Frenchman was staying in the Hogan of one of his close Navajo friends. (Latour was criticized by some of the wealthy Mexican ranchers for his friendliness toward Indians and "Yankees.") As Cather describes this time: "[He] found his Navajo house favorable for reflection, for recalling the past and planning the future.... The Hogan was isolated like a ship's cabin on the ocean, with the murmuring of great winds about it."

The Morning, the Morning!

I find the same true of my own Hogan along San Isabel Creek, ten miles away from the town of Crestone. Though it is larger and sturdier than the original Navajo version, wood-paneled and carpeted, with large windows and cushioned benches, it retains some of the traditional features: an octagon built of rough-hewn logs, with the door facing east to let in the sacred morning light.

Over the years it has become more and more crucial for me to live in a house that lets in full morning light, from which

I draw great strength. I've never been able to articulate exactly why, though of course it connects me to Christ, the Morning Star, Radiant Dawn, and Dayspring from on High, as he is variously called.

Here's how Cather puts it: "In New Mexico he always awoke a young man;... His first consciousness was a sense of the light wind blowing in through the windows, with the fragrance of hot sun and sage-brush; a wind that made one's body feel light and one's heart cry, 'To-day, to-day,' like a child's.... He

did not know just when it had become so necessary to him, but he had come back [from France in old age] to die in exile for the sake of [those lighthearted mornings of the desert.] Something soft and wild and free, something that whispered to the ear on the pillow, lightened the heart, softly, softly picked the lock, slid the bolts, and released the prisoned spirit of man into the wind, into the blue and gold, into the morning, into the morning!"

This Hogan is the perfect morning house with its east window and full glass door; the perfect afternoon house with its south window; the perfect evening house with its west windows. I need all this light, this spacious landscape and spacious skyscape, moonlit and studded with stars, far away from any human habitation and manmade artificial light to spoil the natural light and the natural dark.

Chop Wood, Carry Water

I have such a deep hunger and thirst for the stillness and simplicity of a desert life. The Hogan gives me the most natural earthy rhythms: hauling water, stacking firewood, lighting candles and kerosene lamps after sunset. And the view from the door of the outhouse, which I always keep open, is one of the best in the world!

Though I have to work hard here because of the solitude and rugged wilderness, I try to live balanced days without pressure. This Hogan "magic" helps me become more finely attuned to a deep sense of Presence. Yes, the holy archbishop has something to say about this, too: "But when he entered his study [my Hogan], he seemed to come back to reality, to the sense of a Presence awaiting him. The curtain of the arched doorway had scarcely fallen behind him when...a sense of loss was replaced by a sense of restoration. He sat down before his desk, deep in reflection. It was just this solitariness of love in which a [person's] life could be like his Master's. It was not a solitude of atrophy, of negation, but of perpetual flowering."

Presence and reflection, restoration and flowering, in the silence and solitude of a wilderness hermitage, a desert Hogan, all in the name of Love. This sums up the meaning of my life.

8
Desert Hospitality

Holy Vaudeville

James Foy

Anthony, the ninety-year-old anchorite and resister of temptations, through strange signs and wonders, is led to visit one even older than himself, Paul the hermit, until then only a vague legend among the Desert Fathers. After an arduous desert journey followed by pleadings and persistence, Anthony is finally admitted to the hermit's small domain. Paul has lived in austere seclusion for more than sixty years.

"How Fares the Human Race?"

With human pity and saintly charity, Paul welcomes his visitor, and they exchange the kiss of peace. "Behold, you see before you a man who will soon be dust." He is shaggy and pale, with limbs wasted by extreme age. "Yet because love endures all things, tell me how fares the human race and its cities? What empire rules the kingdoms?" Anthony tells him what little he knows, for he has lived long in hermitage himself.

Double Rations

Then after blessed conversation, a raven comes to settle on a branch of a tree and softly glides down to deposit a loaf of bread before their marveling eyes. "God has sent us our dinner, our merciful, compassionate Lord. It has been thus since I have lived here, but only half a loaf each day. Christ has provisioned his soldiers with double rations this day."

After they give thanks to God, they sit beside a crystal spring. A kind of vaudeville takes place. Who shall break the bread? After you, Alphonse. No, after you, Gaston. This business goes on for a while. Paul insists on the right of his guest. Anthony defers to Paul's seniority. Then each takes hold of an end of the loaf and pulls. Presto!

After eating the bread, they drink a little water, holding their mouths to the spring. They offer to God the Psalm of Praise. They pass the night in vigil.

This story is found in Saint Jerome's Life of Paul *from the fourth century and adapted from a translation by Helen Waddell. At the ancient monastic sites of Kells and Castledermot in Ireland, I have seen high Celtic crosses with carved reliefs of Paul the hermit, Anthony of the Desert, and the raven descending with Eucharistic bread. These first monks were thus honored by Irish monks of a later century, who saw the Desert Fathers as examples and teachers of the dedicated life. Irish monasticism had its "green deserts." The Irish word* diseart *[dee-shirt] translates as "hermitage" or "place of retreat."*

9
Blessings Drop by Drop

Dust Devils and Rock Friends

Tessa Bielecki

"I can't help laughing," says the girl when they ask her, "Aren't you lonely out there with just desert around you?" She then sings about her desert companions: hawks, lizards and coyotes, hot sand, rocky trails, deep canyons, and birds nesting in the cactus, who "sing out over a thousand thorns because they're where they want to be."

The girl is where she wants to be, too, with her "strong brown people" who "have to see mountains and have to see deserts every day... or they don't feel right." (I don't feel right either.) Where else would Desert People want to be? Their land is "no place for anyone who wants soft hills and meadows and everything green, green, green."

If you're a desert person as I am, you'll love the lyrical prose-poems of Byrd Baylor, who has teamed for decades with illustrator Peter Parnall to create an evocative series of children's books I often use for meditation. For Baylor, the spirit, not material things, is necessary for personal development. "Once you make that decision," she wrote from her home in Arivaca, Arizona, "Your whole life opens up and you begin to know what matters and what doesn't."

Parnall lives on a farm in verdant Maine yet has an exquisite feel for the arid desert. His illustrations are simple line drawings, usually with big vibrant splashes of gold, yellow, and red which mirror the light of the desert. Only occasionally does he use green and blue and purple.

Slow Songs to Squash

In *The Desert Is Theirs*, Baylor describes how desert people learn to be patient because "the desert has its own kind of time (that doesn't need clocks)." "Rain is a blessing counted drop by drop." Desert plants don't have to waste moisture on "floppy green leaves." Some can wait three years to bloom. The saguaro cactus can last a whole year after one summer storm. "Squash tastes best if you've sung it slow songs while it's growing." Most importantly, as this volume concludes, "every desert thing knows when the time comes to celebrate."

"What's worth a celebration?" asks the girl who voices Baylor's desert values. She answers for us all: something worth remembering the rest of our lives, that makes us feel like we're standing on top of a mountain, makes our hearts pound, and our breath catch like we're breathing some new kind of air.

"I'm in Charge of Celebrations"

If we're sensitive enough to the sacred all around us, the number of our celebrations multiplies. One year the little girl gave herself 108 celebrations!—"besides the ones that they close school for." These included the days she saw a triple rainbow, seven dust devils "dancing in time to their own windy music," and stars falling from the night sky when she felt her own heart shoot out of her. She celebrated the days when the clouds appeared a rare green and she looked into the eyes of a coyote and knew "I never will feel quite the same again."

She reminds us that some of the best celebrations are "sudden surprises," so we need to pay attention and spend more time outside, "looking around." "What if I'd been in the house? Or what if I hadn't looked up when I did? What if I'd missed it?" What a tragedy!

The girl has the true contemplative spirit natural to a child and essential for every adult: "Unless you become like little children..." (Matthew 18:3). She does not arbitrarily celebrate New Year's on January 1 but in the spring when her favorite cactus blooms because "it always makes me think I ought to bloom myself." On that day she visits all the places she likes to "check how everything is doing." And like our Creator on the Seventh Day, she spends this new day "admiring things."

Everybody Needs a Rock

She pays special attention to rocks, because "everybody needs a rock"—as a friend. She gives us rules for finding such a rock-friend. We must look it right in the eye. It must not be too big or too small, but the perfect size to fit in one hand or a pocket. It must be the perfect color and "look good by itself in the bathtub." Above all, we must choose the rock when everything is quiet, and we must choose it alone. As a lifetime collector of rocks, this child has taught me the best way to find them.

The Way to Start a Day

In *The Way to Start a Day*, Baylor enriches her usual southwestern focus by showing how people all over the world celebrate the sunrise. They "go outside and face the east and greet the sun with some kind of blessing or chant or song that you make yourself and keep for early morning." Peruvians with chants and Aztecs with flutes, Congolese with drums and Chinese with bells, East Indians bathing in the Ganges with marigolds—peoples everywhere and throughout history understand: "A morning needs to be sung to. A new day needs to be honored." These people know they need to make offerings: gold or flowers, fire, feathers, sacred smoke blown to the four directions, or simple good thoughts.

When the sun rises, "all the power of life is in the sky." So we need to welcome the sun, "make it happy," "make a good day for it" and "a good world for it to live in." If the sky turns a color sky never was before, we must simply watch it. "That's part of the magic. That's the way to start a day."

And that's the way to live our lives: in stillness and contemplation, deeply grateful, aware of the sacredness of all things and our kinship with all life.

10
Steward of the West

An "Interview" with Ned Danson

Tessa Bielecki

Instead of a formal review of Edward Bridge Danson: Steward of the West, *a biography by Eric Penner Haury, Ned Danson's grandson, I opted for a more imaginative "interview" with my old friend in the present tense. All the questions are in my own voice. Ned's responses are taken accurately from Haury's book with the exceptions of Jessica's eightieth birthday, my move to Sedona, and the tale of my living in Juliana hermitage.*

Tessa Bielecki: Ned, we both were born and raised in the lush green East, yet you and I share a passion for the arid Arizona desert. When did your love affair with the desert begin?

Ned Danson: I first saw Arizona in 1926 when my family traveled to the Southwest from Cincinnati. My memories of that trip are faint, yet I recall the Grand Canyon, Indian dances, and visits to various archeological sites. But at age ten, I was more interested in the big cars we drove!

T: That changed on your second visit to the desert?

N: In 1937, at age twenty-one, I drove to Arizona to help my uncle turn some desert land south of Tucson into a dude ranch. As we drove out of the canyon west of Bisbee and up on to the plateau to Tombstone at 5 A.M., there was a pink and blue pre-sunrise sky with fleecy white clouds, a hill with a coyote on it. I know it's melodramatic, but that's the way it was. I fell in love with Arizona there and knew it was going to be my home.

T: Arizona was even part of your "marriage proposal" to Jessica, right?

N: On our first date I said, "You're going to love Arizona." She thought, "Wow, what a line!" I wasn't engaged for a while, but doing my darndest to be. My only worry was whether Jess would like Arizona and like going on expeditions and roughing it. She'd "camped out," but never "lived out." There's a big, big difference. But she loved the open. She was a good sport with a sense of humor. And she had imagination and intelligent interest, all necessary attributes.

T: And did she fall in love with the Arizona desert, too?

N: She did. We were married in 1942. After serving in World War II as a naval ensign, we bought a house in Tucson in 1945. Then I got my Ph.D. in Anthropology at Harvard. For my dissertation, I surveyed the Upper Gila River Basin, 14,500 square miles of wilderness along the Arizona-New Mexico border. For three summers, while Jess lived in California with her parents and our two children, I filled in the archeological map. I taught briefly at the University of Colorado in Boulder where I felt I should get excited by Plains archeology. But I never did. The Southwest was always my cup of tea. In 1950 I was asked to teach at the University of Arizona in Tucson, and we moved onto five acres of Sonoran desert. With few houses nearby, we could look out on the desert and walk there whenever we wanted. Our son Ted developed a passion for horseback riding. Our daughter Jan loved playing "knights" with long, straight "ribs" of dead saguaro cactus as lances. Jessica loved wild nature and thrilled to Arizona's powerful thunderstorms. One day, when she heard thunder crashing outside, she threw open the door, and called out, "Isn't this glorious?"

T: She didn't like moving to Flagstaff in northern Arizona?

N: Not at first. I joined the Board of Trustees of the Museum of

Northern Arizona in 1953. In 1956 the Museum needed a new assistant director. Jessica asked who should be named, and I was suggested. For years she considered asking the question one of her worst mistakes. I served as assistant director from 1956-1958 and then director from 1959-1975. Jessica and I especially loved the annual Hopi Show which stimulated a market for the tribe's arts and crafts so that their traditional skills would not be lost—pottery, jewelry, rugs, baskets, *katsina* dolls.

T: **Jessica played a big part in your work, didn't she?**

N: She typed up everything I wrote for my dissertation, and we edited it together. As well as entertaining guests from the Museum, Jessica cleaned cabins for summer assistants and took care of sick staff. As one student wrote years later, "Jessica was an essential presence, providing a depth and beauty of character and spirit that nourished us all." I was energized by the entertaining and loved playing host. But it began to drain Jessica. You know how she loved her solitude. Yet she felt bound to give hospitality—both by a sense of duty and her own inborn desire to give of herself.

T: **Which brings us to Sedona, Arizona, where we met.**

N: All the entertaining got harder for Jessica. In one year alone, we had five hundred guests. When they stayed overnight, Jessica missed her solitude in the tiny chapel she'd created in the house. Without this quiet time, she felt her life was out of balance. In 1969, her sister moved to Sedona and Jess started to visit her. Since you moved to Sedona yourself in 1967 to join the Spiritual Life Institute, you remember how small the town was then, with only 2700 residents. In 1971, Jessica discovered "Singing Waters," and soon after we bought the house with its beautiful gardens, apple orchard, and frontage on Oak Creek.

T: **Getting to know you and Jessica during those years remains one of the highlights of my life.**

N: Jessica found the Spiritual Life Institute's contemplative Christianity invigorating and became such an eager friend of all you "Nadans," as she loved to call you. I wasn't initially drawn to your community. At first I resisted, but as I got to know you all, I changed my thinking—changed it completely.

T: **At the end of your life, did you experience the "desert of human diminishment?"**

N: My health started to decline. Decades of smoking gave me emphysema and heart problems. I had a hard time giving up cigarettes and even deceived Jessica about quitting. And my memory was fading. I could easily use my charm and social skills to cover up my growing forgetfulness, but details were starting to slip. In 1974, the Board of Trustees and I decided it was time for me to retire as director of the Museum.

T: **You stayed involved for almost twenty-five more years?**

N: After retirement I became President of the Board of Trustees and continued to use my skills to help the Museum without having to deal with day-to-day details. Jessica and I made plans to move to Sedona full time and designed an extra wing to turn Singing Waters into a year-round house. It became a living reliquary of our lives. We covered the floors with Navajo rugs, built a special shelf for our Hopi pots and baskets, and hung the walls with Jeffrey Lungé's Southwest paintings. And we added a small chapel for Jessica, where you also came to pray with us.

T: **But you couldn't "save" Sedona, however, and that forced us to move the Spiritual Life Institute to Colorado.**

N: Like you, I felt strongly that the loss of Sedona's scenic area would be a loss for all Americans. With other Sedonans, I tried to make part of Sedona a National Park, but failed. So I joined Keep Sedona Beautiful, and in the 1980s we "saved" three national wilderness areas near Sedona. But I didn't save the land around the Spiritual Life Institute, so Arizona lost you to Colorado.

T: Despite the distance, we remained close friends.

N: Yes, we loved our regular visits to Crestone, and loved building Juliana, the first hermitage for you there. I love how it reminded you of our Sedona home. And I'm glad you got to "christen" it and live there for several months, alone at the new Nada, while the chapel and other hermitages were being built. It was deeply meaningful for Jess and me, members of the Episcopal Church since birth, to convert to Roman Catholicism under the Spiritual Life Institute's influence, and renew our wedding vows with you in Colorado. And we celebrated Jess's eightieth birthday there, too.

T: Among life's many rewards and awards, you also suffered increasing diminishment.

N: In 1987 I had a heart attack. By 1994, Jessica noticed that my memory was seriously failing. That year I fell and suffered a back injury that never fully healed. After I broke my ribs falling into the irrigation ditch at Singing Waters, I required supplemental oxygen full time. I could still tell tales

from my youth, yet I had difficulty recalling what happened that very day. And I loved the southwestern desert until the day I died.

Postscript

Ned Danson died on November 30, 2000. I remember him most as a big barrel-chested bear of a man with a generous heart and a hearty laugh which "injected something special into any and every situation." I last saw him only two months before when I slept outside Singing Waters under a huge cottonwood tree, watching the desert stars as an owl hooted over the rose garden Ned had tended so lovingly. The entire Spiritual Life Institute community was there. Knowing that both Ned and Jessica were nearing the end of their lives, we "anointed" them in a moving outdoor ceremony.

Jessica died five years later on January 11, 2006. Thanks to her daughter, Jan Haury, I had the privilege of sitting with Jessica for the ten days of her dying. You may read my account of this profound "desert experience" on page 149.

Although Ned did not live through the enormous changes that took place in the Spiritual Life Institute after 2003, Jessica did. She witnessed the creation of the Desert Foundation and blessed our efforts. The year before she died, from January through September 2005, she wrote us these words of encouragement: "Fr. Dave and Tessa, You both are such a breath of fresh air and such an inspiration and nourishment for my soul, it is always hard to say goodbye to you. You live so fully—it delights me.... I think your discernment in leaving the Spiritual Life Institute is a very wise choice and the only way for you to go. I'm excited about the future for both of you. You are so dear and thoughtful to keep us posted on your new Desert Foundation. We are thrilled to hear how everything has unfolded so beautifully."

11
Stop, Look, and Listen

A Retreat in the Sonoran Desert

Tessa Bielecki

"Speak, Lord, your servant is listening" (1 Samuel 3:9). Your servant is listening. I am "listening" with the "ears" of my heart, as St. Benedict said. Exhausted not only from this heavily-peopled trip to Arizona, but from the busyness of the past weeks, I walk at dusk in the desert, swim in the moonlight, and sleep nine hours.

May 21: Lizards and Quail

I begin my first full day of retreat with a visit to the Blessed Sacrament and a simple breakfast alone. I start to weep when I see the brown Franciscan habit, so like the Carmelite habit, worn by the old lay brother eating alone at his round table.

I take a morning walk through the desert, listen to the mourning doves, and watch the abundant wildlife: fat lizards, much larger than the ones in Sedona, pairs of quail with their funny "top knots," scampering cottontail rabbits, and a burrow of small rodents I can't see close enough to identify: prairie dogs? ground squirrels? kangaroo rats? Listening to the doves, listening with the ears of my heart.

I sit outside by Our Lady of Guadalupe, young cottonwoods in front of her, a luscious purple jacaranda tree behind. Too much maintenance noise begins, and workers make no effort to be quiet, as though this were a mere hotel and not a retreat center. A golf cart delivers fresh linen, a man in a bright red shirt cleans the pool, another in a straw hat runs one of those horrible blowers to clear the patio of jacaranda blossoms. "Such a dirty tree," I heard one woman lament at breakfast. Dirty? Thank goodness I had already scooped up cupfuls of dried petals and scattered them on my desk.

I recall the old Zen story from *The Book of Tea.* A young monk raked up all the fallen leaves from the stone garden and smoothed all the gravel. The Zen master arrived, shook the red maple tree, and a new crop of autumn leaves fell over the freshly swept paths. "Ah!" he said.

Immersed in all this desert beauty, yellow palo verde blossoms falling to the ground around the cactus behind me, I begin to weep again out of grief over my loss of Arizona, the desert, my Carmelite community.

Our Lady of Guadalupe

To escape the noise, I move to the other side of the Guadalupe mosaic with red roses painted on the wall. The top of a cross with two human arms: Christ's left hand pierced with a nail, the right hand of St. Francis pierced with the stigmata. And a prayer: *Mater Misericordiae, Madre de Misericordia, Mother of Mercy, Pray for us.*

A fresco of Juan Diego "preaching to his people" with Guadalupe on his *tilma*, a shower of roses fallen to the ground at his feet. But the people look more white than Indian, and Juan Diego more like an entitled conquistador than indigenous peasant. *Madre de Misericordia, pray for us.*

A fountain splashes in front of me. A flock of yellow finches comes to drink, and emerald hummingbirds, until a red-tailed hawk swoops in and scares them away. I let the jacaranda purple fall all over me—until the inevitable bird poop splats on my right shoulder and I move!

I remember all over again that I often pray best with a pen in my hand.

I eat a big salad for lunch in a noisy dining room, crowded with talkative staff. Then I return to the tiny Blessed Sacrament Chapel to read and pray. But in the cool sunless quiet, I begin to fall asleep, so I stretch out on my bed for a quick catnap before a special Mass at 2 P.M. My fatigue is so great, probably also affected by the one-hundred-degree heat, that I sleep over two hours, missing Mass, and wake disoriented by strange but healing dreams I cannot remember. Ice cold water to revive me, then out again to Our Lady of Guadalupe and a lovely breeze under the cottonwoods. Through a break in the trees I revel in the earth tones of small rocky Mummy Mountain to the north, with one stately saguaro standing sentinel.

Sunset and Moon Shadows

Another walk at sunset along the oleander hedge rows, past the elegant eucalyptus and the ubiquitous creosote bushes, at this time of year in their fuzzy "cotton ball" stage. I explore the mimosa trees with their ferny leaves and pale yellow catkins, dropping their delicate confetti blossoms on the ground. I once heard that mimosa leaves curl up when you touch them, but these never move as I stroke them.

I meet more birds and rabbits, and this evening, after quail couples all day long, a covey of babies scurrying under the bushes. I sit where I can see the western sky glow and the colors change on Camelback Mountain, which looks more like a sleeping giant from this angle. I have been outdoors all day, except for meals and my nap. What a marvel! I love communing deeply with this patch of desert, the landscape nourishing my soulscape.

By 8 P.M. it's too dark to read, so I rest my head and watch the stars "come out," surrounding the waxing moon, now half-full. I remember my first moonlit night in the Sedona desert over forty years ago when I was awestruck by its brightness and "heard" my Indian name: Moon Shadow. (Then Cat Stevens wrote his famous song!) I sit so still, such a part of the desert, a kangaroo rat almost walks over my foot.

The tallest trees rustle their leaves, a soft breeze caresses my face. The sounds of traffic on the road diminish this far back from the retreat house buildings, but I hear planes taking off from Sky Harbor Airport, neighborhood children playing and screaming, and way across the street, loud music from a suburban party. I long for the pristine silence of the real wilderness around my Crestone hermitage.

May 22: A Roadrunner

After a hot still morning, the wind has picked up like yesterday. I sit in the shade of a gorgeous palo verde tree: leaves small and waxy to prevent the evaporation of moisture, with thoroughly green branches and trunk. The yellow blossoms have a stunning orange center.

I see more of the little rodents but will have to wait till I get home to "name" them—much smaller than our Colorado prairie dogs. I spook myself thinking about rattlesnakes but see no signs of any. I wonder about the purpose of the quail's floppy top knot and love the russet color of the male's head. And then I see what I've been longing for: a roadrunner. I follow him as long as I can, till he disappears in the dried and rattling brittle-bush. Another desert theophany!

There's a big used book sale going on this weekend, and for a while I get lost in it, unable to resist the bargain prices for *St. Francis* by Nikos Kazantzakis, hard covers of Mary Stewart's Merlin novels which I'm currently rereading, Huston Smith's classic on world religions, Joseph Campbell and Bill Moyers on the power of myth, a life of St. Edmund Campion, the Jesuit "Scarlet Pimpernel," Charles de Foucauld and desert stuff, and for only fifty cents each, a few paperback duplicates of books I've read and now can cut up instead of the more laborious process of taking notes.

I also can't resist a tiny volume of the liturgy of St. John Chrysostom, since I love his Easter Sermon so much. I can't find Murray Bodo's *The Journey and the Dream*, which affected me profoundly when I came upon it in Assisi on a pivotal day of my pilgrimage there in 2004. But I find Bodo's little fictionalized life of St. Clare, which even includes a meditation on Camelot, very much on my mind these days of immersion in Merlin, King Arthur, and the Knights of the Round Table. I realize that

I haven't read enough these past months and look forward to more when I get home.

Lunch today is pork green chili, black beans, and a lovely flan with fresh strawberries and kiwi fruit. All the meals here are healthy and beautifully prepared, and it's a treat not to have to cook for myself. This is not a place to lose weight. But I'm walking over ten thousand steps a day and swimming fifty minutes, too.

What a racket tonight when I went out for a "quiet" sunset. There was an outdoor concert not far away at El Chorro Restaurant. I didn't mind the Indian drums and chanting, but when the rock 'n' roll started, I went back to my room and the "white noise" of my primitive air conditioner.

May 23: Feast of Pentecost

I woke at 5:30 A.M. today, a sign of how rested I feel, full of renewed energy. I went out immediately to enjoy the desert in the cool of morning and couldn't get over the different feel on my skin. I watched a dove perched on top of the lavish creamy blossoms of a saguaro cactus and then saw something I've read about for years but never observed in the wild: a cactus wren nesting in a hole in the saguaro. Now if I could only see a furry black tarantula, my desert menagerie would be complete.

I went back to the book sale before it even opened and found a new table of spiritual books, and there was the treasure: *The Journey and the Dream*! I'll save it for back home as I prepare for my October talk on St. Francis.

I intended to go to a later Mass today for this special feast and was surprised to find that the early one at 7:15 A.M. featured a full choir and a band with piano, two guitars, and a complete set of drums, including congas, so I went to that. It was a vibrant liturgy, with good participation by the congregation, and a fine homily. But it was a little too upbeat for me with chairs set up outside, children running around, and a TV screen broadcasting the Mass to folks out on the lawn. My favorite part was singing the *Sanctus* in Spanish, Polish, Tongan, and Tagalog and the *Agnus Dei* in Vietnamese, to commemorate the many "tongues" of Pentecost. ("Amen" in Tagalog is *sumasampalataya!*)

Today was particularly "zoo-y" here. Three masses blasted outdoors over loud speakers, people milling around and visiting everywhere, youth group meeting in a neighboring building. It's clear that in order to survive, this center has opted for conferences, educational programs, and parish activities over its former retreat emphasis from the years when I lived in Sedona. I made good use of the time and space but wouldn't come here again on retreat, only to write and enjoy the desert, as well as the accommodations made reasonable by superb meals and a great pool. (I spent a lot of today swimming vigorously, since there wasn't much quiet.)

At 7 P.M. I heard the Pentecost music start up again and wanted to sing in all those languages once more. It was good to celebrate more than one Mass on such a major feast, as we do at Christmas and Easter. Pentecost has always been a favorite of mine. And we get to use red vestments!

May 24: Time to Go

I felt my energy shift this morning and knew I was ready to leave this place. I finished reading Jean Houston's *Search for the Beloved,* checked out of my room, packed the car, made a last visit to the Blessed Sacrament and what had become "my" beloved patch of desert. There's a labyrinth there, and I decided to walk it as my last meditation. Since this particular labyrinth features seven circuits, and this year I am completing the first seven-year cycle of leaving the Spiritual Life Institute, I thought it would be a fitting end to my retreat.

As I was leaving, I saw the old Franciscan brother raking leaves near the labyrinth and simply had to speak to him and thank him for the witness of his silent prayerful presence. He was beautiful and agreed that this place has become too noisy since he arrived in 1965, just two years before I went to Sedona.

He said he loves to be outside doing manual labor in the desert garden because he can "stop, look, and listen". Otherwise he gets caught up in the superficial talk and loses his recollection. "Say a little prayer for me, Tessa," were his final words. He was the most inspiring person I'd seen here.

I had no agenda for these days and no expectations. The retreat was exactly what I needed: stillness and simplicity, rest and reflection, a profound reconnection with the Sonoran Desert, and most important of all: deeply living in the moment.

Part 2
The Tent of Meeting

If I do not discover in myself the terrain where the Hindu, the Muslim, the Jew and the atheist may have a place—in my heart, in my intelligence, in my life—I will never be able to enter into a genuine dialogue.

Raimon Panikkar

12
Your People and Your Land

A Walled Sanctuary

David Denny

Ever since moving into my new hermitage called *al Hadiyah,* Arabic for "the gift," I have greeted visitors with my favorite Arabic greeting: *Ahlan wa sahlan,* which means, roughly translated, "These are your people and may this be your welcoming land."

You step into my entry gallery onto a red and black carpet given to me in 1970 in Afghanistan. I was an exchange student there, and despite having learned in my orientation not to compliment Afghans on their belongings, I blurted out one day in my family's home in Herat, "What a beautiful rug!" The next thing I knew, it was mine.

That's part of the Afghan code of hospitality: if a guest admires a possession, the host gives it away, even if it costs the owner dearly. Although I felt some sheepishness accepting the gift, I am grateful. I could not have known at age seventeen how profoundly my life would be shaped by those months in a Muslim household halfway around the world.

Contemplative Christianity

As I went on to college, I felt drawn to contemplative Christianity, a tradition that was willing to listen to and learn from other cultures and religions. I discovered Trappist monk and writer Thomas Merton and Bede Griffiths, the English Benedictine monk who founded a Christian ashram in India.

I hungered for a Christianity that reflected the wide-open arms of Jesus, the Jewish rabbi whom I believe is the embodiment of God. I found no condemnation of the "other" in the Gospel. On the contrary, Jesus shocked friend and foe by his openness to the "other," the alien, the "un-chosen," and communicated a sense of truth through communion and compassion, not through the unilateral imposition of an ideology.

Having studied Arabic and Islam in college, I put my interest in the other Abrahamic traditions aside for decades as I deepened my immersion in the Carmelite tradition and the Christian mystics. But after 9/11 and a seismic shift in my own vocation, I longed to return to the teachings and history of the other Abrahamic traditions. When Tessa Bielecki and I created the Desert Foundation and I found myself in a new house, a blank canvas, I began to dream about what kind of Middle Eastern art might surround me in this new life.

Spirituality and Matter

Some may imagine that spirituality is not about matter. But Jesus loved lilies, good food and friendship, wine and walking under the sun and stars. In fact, according to John the Evangelist, Jesus incarnated the Word and the Word loved these worldly wonders into being. I recall a poem, "Things," by Spanish poet Gloria Fuertes: "These things, our things, / how they want to be wanted! / ...the door asks to be opened and closed, / the wine to be purchased and drunk,..."

I wanted my door to open to a world, not just a house, to things that mean beauty to me, images that want to be wanted, that want to tell stories. I wanted to bring together manifestations of beauty from peoples separated by conflict: the sons and daughters of Abraham, our father in faith. Even if for now we cannot or will not live together in peace and justice, I wanted the work of our hands to share a common ground, to suggest a premonition of reconciliation.

Solitude and Hospitality

The first art you see when crossing the threshold of *al Hadiyah* is an embroidered cloth with shimmering red geometrical patterns on a black background, woven by women from Beit Jala, a village near Bethlehem. Its dominant colors are the same as the Afghan rug, and although Afghanistan is far from Palestine, and its culture is not Semitic, the patterns of the textiles share similarities. Many Palestinians of the West Bank and Gaza Strip cannot enter Jerusalem, so a nonprofit called *Sunbula* gathers Palestinian crafts for sale at a shop sponsored by St. Andrew's Church in Jerusalem.

Above the weaving hangs an ornate sign proclaiming *ahlan wa sahlan* in Arabic calligraphy, crafted by Shahna Lax, our Jewish friend in Crestone. The greeting may be Arabic, but it belongs to no single religion or scripture. It is a simple offering of the hospitality that reigns throughout the Middle East with roots in desert Bedouin traditions. I want to offer that kind of hospitality in my home, even though I live as a solitary.

The wall includes a small Persian miniature of nine men meeting on a verdant hillside. A white pony stands in the foreground beside a stream. Like my rug, it reminds me of Afghanistan.

I remember standing with my Afghan "brother," Syed Ahmad, one evening years ago at a place called Bagha Bala (High Garden) outside Kabul. The heat of the day waned; a breeze blew through the fruit trees; the lights of kerosene lamps began to appear from within the flat-roofed adobe homes below us. The full moon rose, and I felt I was inside a Persian miniature, a landscape and atmosphere that, until that moment, would have seemed purely fictional to me, a son of the green flat farmlands of northern Indiana.

Pottery and Paradise

Three ceramic plates hang on the wall. Made by Christian potters in Palestine, one is glazed with the Our Father in Arabic. I have memorized the first verse of the Qur'an; it's time I memorized the Our Father in Arabic. A simple blue and black floral pattern covers a smaller dish, testifying to desert dwellers' fascination with flowers and gardens: a reminder that our word "paradise" comes from the Persian word for garden. A stately white camel stands in silhouette against a floral background on the third plate.

This reminds me of March 2000, when I rode a camel for two days in the desert of Wadi Rum, near Aqaba, Jordan. Seated high on the camel's back, I wandered through a maze of sun-drenched and shadowed red cliffs on sands that shifted from beige to ochre to rust. Spring rains allowed tiny wildflowers to spring up in impossible crannies of sand and stone. Before and after my little expedition, my teen-aged camel driver's mother sat me down next to her charcoal fire in her enclosed patio to drink sweet hot tea spiced with sage.

But the camel also reminds me of the Jewish tradition, of the sojourn in Sinai, and Isaiah's vision of the day when all nations will come to Jerusalem, drawn by the truth and light it radiates:

Then you will see and be radiant,
And your heart will thrill and rejoice;
Because the abundance of the sea will be turned to you,
The wealth of the nations will come to you.
A multitude of camels will cover you,
The young camels of Midian and Ephah;
All those from Sheba will come;
They will bring gold and frankincense,
And will bear good news of the praises of the Lord.
(Isaiah 60:5-6)

45

Sanctuary, Not Separation

You also see a primitive image of the Holy Family on the wall, which reminds me of my time in Egypt in August 2004. It was a very difficult season in my life, and visits to Coptic churches and some of the oldest Christian monasteries on earth, as well as the generous companionship of my old friend, Gary Nabhan, helped me find my way forward.

The image is painted on a small sheet of gold-fibered papyrus with an Arabic caption announcing "the entry of Our Lord into Egypt with his mother and Joseph the carpenter." Egyptian Coptic Christians trace their origins to St. Mark the Evangelist and have a lively devotion to the Holy Family, who found shelter in Egypt during Jesus' infancy.

The trip to Egypt also introduced me to Christians living as a minority in a predominantly Muslim country. I sensed the tensions as well as the possibilities for reconciliation that come from centuries sharing a common homeland.

On the center of the bookshelf as you enter lies a worn and empty basket. It comes from the Egyptian oasis of Siwa, an ancient settlement visited by Alexander the Great before there were Christians or Muslims. The basket is tattered but tightly woven. I like to think it holds nothing but Promise.

A wall can be a terrible thing. I want the wall that people see when entering my home to be a sign not of separation, but of sanctuary, protection, hospitality. I want it to show that beauty is not monopolized by one tradition, but shared by all. I want it to show you what Paradise might look like through the prism of my desert sojourns with Jews, Muslims, and Christians in our troubled Abrahamic family.

13
A Tribute to My Rebbe

The Father of Jewish Renewal

Tessa Bielecki

R abbi Zalman Schachter-Shalomi was born August 17, 1924 in Zholkiew, Poland and died in Boulder, Colorado on July 3, 2014, almost reaching his ninetieth birthday.

I first met my "Rebbe" in July of 2004, when we both spoke at a conference on death and dying in Aspen. I was "dying" myself at the time, an excruciating interior death from post-traumatic-stress disorder as a result of leaving the Spiritual Life Institute community after almost forty years (a story for another time). Reb Zalman called me regularly for over a year, simply to ask how I was feeling. Then he invited me to his home to celebrate the Jewish Passover and my own personal Passover from death to new life. When my father died in 2008, Reb Zalman visited my hermitage in Crestone and said special blessings in both Hebrew and Polish.

A True Holy of Holies

The Rebbe had a Prayer Room in his basement: a true "Holy of Holies," small, dark, mysterious, and filled with what I affectionately called "Jewish stuff." I loved to pray there together with him. We usually sat in silence, in the deep contemplative Presence where all religious traditions meet. He'd end by singing in Hebrew. I didn't know the words in that ancient language, but my heart soared, and I understood the meaning behind the words.

One morning, at the discussion group Reb Zalman gathered weekly in his library, I spoke about Mt. Carmel, outside of modern Haifa in Israel, a site sacred to both Jews and Christians. The prophet Elijah, who lived on Mt. Carmel, is the "spiritual father" of all Carmelites. Sixteenth-century Carmelite, St. John of the Cross, describes the whole spiritual journey as an "Ascent of Mt. Carmel," also the title of one of his great mystical works.

That day the Rebbe asked me to talk instead about a deeper and more interior connection between Christians and Jews, the mysterious realm of "bridal mysticism" described in the *Song of Songs*, where we experience God not as Lord or Creator, not even as father, mother, or brother, but as our Divine Spouse. (I have written extensively about this in *Holy Daring*.)

Reb Zalman was the visionary father of the Jewish Renewal Movement, holder of the World Wisdom Chair at Naropa University, author of numerous books, including *From Age-ing to Sage-ing*, an innovator in ecumenical dialogue, and a spiritual revolutionary who infused religion with new vitality and depth.

But I remember "my" Rebbe most for his simple loving kindness, the sign of spiritual authenticity in any religious tradition.

14
Geologist of the Soul

Talks on Rebbe-craft and Spiritual Leadership

Tessa Bielecki

"My rebbe was a geologist of the soul," said the seventh Lubavitcher Rebbe, Rabbi Menachem Mendel Schneerson (1902-1944). "There are so many treasures in the earth: gold, silver, diamonds. But if you don't know where to dig, you'll only find dirt, rocks, and mud. The rebbe can tell you where to dig, and what to dig for, but the digging you must do yourself."

Reb Netanel Miles-Yépez edited *Geologist of the Soul,* a collection of talks by Rabbi Zalman, founder of the Jewish Renewal Movement and one of the world's leading authorities on Hasidism. Reb Zalman discusses Jewish spiritual leadership from the perspective of the Hasidic Rebbe, applying traditional Hasidic models and teachings to contemporary situations.

He covers spiritual guidance, the teacher-student relationship, the efficacy of intercessory prayer, scales of moral and faith development, the House of Hillel (loving-kindness) and the House of Shammai (discipline), the value of spiritual imagination, intuition, mentors, "intimate apprenticeship" and the importance of first being a disciple and not a "spiritual loner." In the discussion of spiritual typologies, I was charmed by the descriptions of Jesus as a "viscerotone," Buddha as a "cerebrotone," and Moses as a "somatotone."

I got confused with some of the Hebrew, the Four Worlds, and the Tree of Life. Otherwise I found a wealth of inspiration in these informal talks. It felt as if I were sitting at Reb Zalman's feet, listening to stories from all the great Hasidic lineages, experiencing Reb Zalman himself as a *butzina kaddisha,* a "holy candle," full of light, wisdom, humor, and compassion. I was touched by the humble accounts of his own painful failures.

The strongest talk is the last, a summary dialogue between the two rebbes. Through Reb Netanel's clear insights and questions, we understand the difference between a rabbi and a Rebbe and a spiritual director and a Rebbe: the Rebbe and his Hasid have a deeper "soul-affinity" and a "contract of intimacy and concern" that ideally focuses on spiritual development yet may also involve "more mundane concerns—children, the cows and the chickens."

Reb Netanel points out that "a Rebbe's mastery is not one of *information*, but of *attunement*." Reb Zalman concludes: "Attunement is not verbal, it's not left brain, so there is no way to write about that or get it through reading alone. No, not everyone can become a Rebbe, and certainly not by education; one needs something from *Above* to fulfill this mission."

Reb Zalman preferred the vocation of the cobbler to the vocation of the prophet. He spent his days stitching the sandals of broken souls and stitching together the shards of misunderstanding that lay scattered around our post–Holocaust world.

Rabbi Shaul Magid

15
Abrahamic Shadows

Seeking to Heal the Damage

David Denny

*W*hen I first saw the title of *Religion Gone Astray: What We Found at the Heart of Interfaith,* I thought it might be ironic: Were the authors saying that to go "astray" is a good thing? After all, engagement in difficult dialogue with other traditions, "straying" into close contact, can be a fruitful, enlightening adventure. A good thing. Although the authors demonstrate the truth of this irony, the book proposes a straightforward thesis: the Abrahamic religions have strayed from their core teachings.

The authors confront the experience of exclusivity, violence, inequality between men and women, and homophobia in Judaism, Christianity and Islam. This book is not for the fainthearted. It is for those who agonize over the tension between these traditions' core teachings and the way these traditions have, for many believers, undermined those central tenets.

Pastor Don Mackenzie, Rabbi Ted Falcon and Imam Jamal Rahman are known to many as "The Three Amigos," friends from Seattle who have spoken and written extensively about the need for interfaith dialogue, especially since 9/11. Each chapter includes each author's experience of his religion's having gone astray, scriptural and institutional support for this inconsistency, informed commentary on this "straying," and reflection on core teachings that may help heal the damage done.

The authors have listened to questions posed by people across the country who attend their presentations on dialogue. They have discussed these questions among themselves, and the book is the fruit of these challenging questions and vulnerable conversations. Their reflections on growing up Jewish, Christian, and Muslim and their encounters with exclusivity, violence, inequality, and homophobia within their lives and traditions help us trust their integrity and their hope for healing and growth found in their faiths' core teachings on oneness, love, and compassion.

Although they treat these heavy topics seriously, the "amigos" also manifest a lightness and humor that makes them attractive. I have met Jamal Rahman and enjoyed this combination of depth and lightheartedness, mystical wisdom and warm approachability.

No single person represents an entire tradition. Roman Catholics, for example, will not find their tradition represented in some of Mackenzie's reflections. Because many Americans are unfamiliar with Islam, and because violence and misogyny are such "hot topics" in today's headlines, it is particularly healing to hear Rahman's open, mystical voice.

In the end, the authors do suggest that "going astray" may be, if not a good thing, at least inevitable, and a catalyst for growth. God forgives, and having received forgiveness, we also receive deepened humility and wisdom.

16
A Lost Treasure

Deir Mar Musa Monastery
Jo L'Abbate

"**A**re you sure you want us to leave you here by yourself?"
The desert sun was setting fast, and our guide looked
up to the monastery from where we stood. The guidebooks
warned against attempting the mile-long scrabble up the
mountain after dark, and he knew I was already weary. I was
part of a special summer program in Arabic at Damascus
University in Syria. The director had carefully chosen an
expert guide for our excursion to the Crusader castles.

We had left the university at 5 A.M. and climbed through
medieval castles all day. The guide's reputation and honor
were at stake, not to mention future business with the
university, if anything happened to me and he wasn't there to
help. Arab peoples take hospitality seriously. I was unsure
myself, but having come this far to visit this remarkable place,
I couldn't turn back now. I decided the "worst-case scenario"
was a chilly night on the path if I couldn't make it all the
way, so acting more confident than I felt, I reassured him and
headed up the path.

I was fortunate. Syrian guidebooks are usually several
years out-of-date, and the monks had completed a mile-long
stairway from the "welcome station," a picnic area with water,
tables, shade and restrooms, to Deir Mar Musa, the sixth-
century monastery where a young monastic community is
restoring the ancient treasures of the building and the tradition
of Christian hospitality.

The Smaller Door

Approaching the end of the stairs, I heard bells calling
for evening prayer. I hurried to the top and saw a tiny door,
perhaps three feet tall. Older homes in Syria were built with

*these doors, usually in the middle of a larger one, and a
gracious guest would choose the smaller door, bending low
to enter the host's home as a sign of humility and respect. I
removed my backpack, tossed it through the door and entered
the enclosure of Deir Mar Musa. Seeing a stack of shoes
outside a door, I removed my own and quietly slipped into the
chapel to find television cameras and a hundred Italian college
students! Italian television was filming a documentary on the
monastery and its founder.*

During a retreat in his formation as a young Jesuit, Fr. Paolo
Dall'Oglio saw the ruins of the ancient monastery of Deir Mar
Musa al-Habashi, St. Moses the Abyssinian, in the Syrian desert
outside the city of Nebek and began to conceive re-founding a
community there. As he discerned the inspiration and purpose
of the community, three tenets emerged: first, the rediscovery
of spiritual life through prayer, silence and contemplation;
second, evangelical simplicity, living in harmony with and full
responsibility for, creation and society; and third, a mission to
serve as "Christian leaven in Islamic dough," emphasizing the
ancient monastic tradition of hospitality.

Fr. Paolo coordinated the efforts of the local Church,
the Syrian government and a group of Arab and European
volunteers, and the restoration work began in 1984. A new
monastic community of men and women from different
churches of the East and West, dependent upon the local Syrian
Catholic tradition, was founded in 1991. Restoration of the
main monastery building was completed in 1994, thanks to
continued cooperation between the governments of Italy and
Syria. This cooperation continued in 2002-2003 with European
help, jointly supporting the establishment of a school to restore
Deir Mar Musa's frescoes.

*In spite of the distracting television crew, evening prayer
seemed to proceed normally. Everyone sat on the floor,*

covered in carpets, or on low benches around the edges of the room. All prayer was in Arabic, the monastery's "official" language, the liturgical language of most of the Oriental Churches, and the universal religious language of the Islamic Community. We knelt and put our foreheads to the ground while chanting the Trisagion *beloved in the Syriac Churches: "Praise to you Holy God! Praise to you All-Powerful God! Praise to you Immortal God! Have mercy on us." We closed with the Our Father, and the large crowd drifted into the courtyard, hungry for dinner. Stools and chairs were brought up, and large trays were set on other stools to serve as tables.*

Radical Hospitality

The monks have one radio phone line which is always busy with the internet, but no reservations or communications are needed for individuals. People simply show up, stay for as long as they like, then leave. The vast majority of visitors are Muslims from the surrounding villages who make a day or evening holiday with their families. This call to "radical hospitality" is an essential component of the community's mission. While the community maintains an ancient Christian presence in the region and assists local Christian communities, they also work closely with the Syrian antiquities authorities and the national museum to preserve the cultural treasures of the ancient sites, and with the agricultural ministry on sustainable agriculture and preservation of the fragile desert ecosystems.

The monks, long-term retreatants, and friends brought out simple but plentiful food from the tiny kitchen. Arabic bread, lebna *(thickened yogurt), olives, home-made cheese from the monastery goats, olive oil and* zatar *(a blend of thyme, sesame seeds, and other herbs) were the staples of every meal. A cooked vegetable dish of squash, beans, and tomatoes rounded out lunch and dinner. Scrambled eggs and the fabulous homemade apricot preserves found throughout Syria were*

Sunday's special treats. Folks walked through the crowded courtyard pouring tea and water.

With the exception of a Fulbright scholar who was an old friend of the community, I was the only American and shared stories with the Italians, Syrians, Germans and Australians at my table. After dinner the tables were put away, the film crew and many people left, but there were still almost fifty people to spend the night. I found Sister Huda, one of the first members of the community and the only woman at that time, and asked if I could stay the night. She asked if I would share a bed. I agreed, and she showed me to a lovely small room at the top of the stairs over the courtyard, which I believe was a "perk" for my age, since twelve of the female college students were in a large adjoining room in bunks, and most of the men rolled out sleeping bags for a night under the Bedouin tent on the second deck over the courtyard. The bell rang for Grand Silence, and I considered the day.

The Christian presence in Syria is palpable. In Damascus, I lived just off the "street called Straight" and two blocks from the house where Ananias cured St. Paul of his blindness. (See Acts of the Apostles 9:10-19.) And now I was standing in a centuries-old monastery, looking out at the desert in union with our Christian forebears, with another desert center dedicated to silent, contemplative presence half a world away in Crestone, Colorado.

The politicians and media want us to believe we are headed for a "clash of civilizations" between the Christian West and the Muslim East. In the midst of this debate, God has inspired two reconciling efforts, one at each of the "poles," at almost the same time, with many of the same interests and very similar spirits. There is hope for our future together, hope that flourishes and flows into our world through Deir Mar Musa and the Desert Foundation.

In Memoriam

In July 2013, Jesuit Fr. Paolo Dall'Oglio, the visionary founder of Deir Mar Musa, was kidnapped in Syria. After more than thirty years there, he was expelled in 2012 for supporting the anti-Assad opposition. This was a controversial stand to take, given that many Syrian Christians have supported Syrian President Bashar al-Assad because some claim he has protected Syrian religious minorities, including Christians, who are about ten percent of the Syrian population. But Dall'Oglio refused to trust Assad's "protection," given the myriad forms of repression his regime promotes.

Fr. Paolo sneaked back into Syria in order to negotiate the release of journalists held by ISIS. This is when he disappeared. One ISIS defector claimed to have seen Fr. Paolo in a Syrian prison, but this claim has not been confirmed. Hind Aboud Kabawat, a long-time friend of Fr. Paolo, says, "We have to follow his principles. To love the others, to build bridges with the others. To cross the line and make peace and make reconciliation. This was his favorite word...The Assad regime wants us to hate the Muslim people, they want the Muslims to hate us. But Father Paolo taught us we must do everything to keep the nation together."

The last post on Deir Mar Musa's web site is a press release dated February 29, 2012. It describes the arrival, one week earlier, of masked, armed men looking for food and money. No one was harmed. These are the release's final words: "We thank God for the protection of his angels, and we prayed during mass for our aggressors and their families. In spite of these painful events, we did not lose our inner peace nor the desire to serve reconciliation." *(D.D.)*

17
Dar al-Islam

Learning to Teach

Tessa Bielecki and David Denny

In July 2010, we attended Dar al Islam's annual Teachers' Institute in Abiquiu, New Mexico. The Institute aims to help American secondary school instructors and other professionals teach about Islam more effectively. If you are a teacher of any kind, you can apply to this all-expenses-paid institute and learn in Abiquiu as well. Visit daralislam.org and click on the Teachers' Institute. The following are excerpts from a blog we took turns writing during our ten-day experience.

July 12, 2010: First Day of Learning

This was an intense first day of learning. We took a tour of the mosque and *madrasa*, "school" in Arabic, which enhanced our appreciation of its classical Muslim architecture. Then class began with a reading from the Qur'an. Because I love color imagery, this was my favorite verse:

> *(Our religion is)*
> *The Colour of Allah:*
> *And who can colour better*
> *Than Allah? And it is He*
> *Whom we worship.*

We then had a lengthy discussion of the challenges of teaching about Islam, including closedmindedness, islamophobia, the differences between classical and current Islam, misinformation, especially from the media, conflicts within Islam itself, and the difference between cultural Islam and fundamental beliefs based on the Qur'an and Islamic Law.

All of us are interested in finding resources from the non-western world and learning how to communicate with those who may automatically condemn Islam. And what do we want to inspire in our students? Mere tolerance? Acceptance? Or something deeper, such as respect and appreciation?

During the afternoon we watched a 2009 film, *New Muslim Cool,* documenting how Puerto Rican rapper Hamza Pérez converted to Islam and turned from drug dealing to drug counseling. There's the "brotherhood of the street," he explained to inmates at the county jail, and an even higher brotherhood of "companionship in God" through which we begin to find that elusive peace within ourselves.

After dinner we had "Arabic 101" with Dr. Muhammad Shafi from Pakistan. We pronounced every letter of the alphabet, not so much to remember it but to "taste" the flavor of the language. We learned that the Qur'an was the first book written down in "book" form instead of scrolls, that Arabic grammar is the first grammar in any language, the Arabic dictionary the first dictionary in any language. The lesson was overwhelming for most of us, especially at the end of the day. I was almost falling asleep but deeply awed by the sophistication, subtlety, and elegance of the language. *(T.B.)*

July 13: America and Mecca

I'm stimulated and exhausted at the end of this day. We began with a lecture on Islam in America by Gambian scholar Sulayman Nyang. He noted the possibility of Muslim contacts with Native Americans in the pre-Columbian era. Some scholars suggest Arabic influences on Native American languages. There are historical accounts of possible voyages across the Atlantic by African Muslim navigators.

From these murky, disputed possibilities, Dr. Nyang moved on through American history since the founding of the United States. I was surprised by the extent of the Muslim presence. Some of us may associate patriotism with a narrow sense of America's Christian moral superiority and pride ourselves on shutting out other "alien" cultures. But America is also the land of wild differences and opportunity for families from every corner of the world, and these stories of Muslim immigrant experiences in the U.S. are a moving part of our American heritage.

Later, Pakistani Islamic scholar Mustansir Mir took us through the cultural context in which Muhammad was born, the first years of his life in Mecca and the beginnings of his prophetic life. Mustansir's voice is mellifluous and spellbinding when he quotes Arabic poetry.

This evening, Susan Douglass of Georgetown University's Prince Alwaleed Bin Talal Center for Muslim-Christian Understanding shared a number of invaluable resources on Muslim art and architecture, Islamic Spain, the cultural history of the Indian Ocean, teaching Islam and other world religions in a fair and balanced way.

While I took a siesta and studied this afternoon, Tessa took some of our new friends to Abiquiu and showed them the penitente *morada*, the beautiful old adobe church, and Georgia O'Keeffe's house. It was in the nineties today, but we also had our first hint of rain. *(D.D.)*

July 14: No Compulsion in Religion

The day began with another remarkable lecture by Susan Douglass, who gave us more helpful resources. We mapped the rise of Islam, distinguishing between the rapid spread of Muslim territory and the gradual growth of Islam as a religion, which coincided with the growth of Christianity and Buddhism.

Do you know that only twelve percent of the world's Muslims are Arabs? And half the population of Africa is Muslim? It's also important to note that the Qur'an specifies: "Let there be no compulsion in religion" (2:256). This verse tells Muslims that they cannot force people to convert to Islam.

Professor Mustansir Mir taught twice today. In the morning he took us through the Medinan period of Muhammad's life. In the evening we explored the Muslim Articles of Faith. He lights

60

up when he quotes the poet Iqbal, whom I don't know. Just as I was about to ask who he was, Fr. Dave beat me to it! Then Mir described Iqbal as one of the most brilliant poet-philosophers in the history of Islam. Naturally Fr. Dave will order the Persian-Urdu anthology, *Tulip in the Desert.*

This is short because we have lots of homework tonight, including Richard Bulliet's essay entitled "The Case for Islamo-Christian Civilization," a subject dear to our own hearts. *(T.B.)*

July 16: Books Piled High

We missed writing yesterday. It was a busy day without a break. During "free time" in the afternoon we met about our group study projects. We had a major question and answer session, and a talk on the links between Judaism, Christianity, and Islam, which focused exclusively on scripture and the prophets. This was excellent, but we had hoped for more spiritual links. The morning session was the most satisfying for us because it focused on Sufism and the inner life of Muslim spirituality and included some beautiful poetry.

After dinner we were unexpectedly invited to a Sufi *dhikr,* an evening of prayer, song, and chant with our friends Benyamin and Rabia Van Hattum at the small neighborhood mosque that we have visited several times before with Colorado College students. After nearly a week of intense "book learning," it was refreshing to set aside the study mind and open up the heart as well as our singing voices. It was a vivid experience of the poem we had heard earlier by Bullhe Shah, the eighteenth-century Punjabi mystic:

> *The books you read...*
> *Are piled around you, and so high!...*
> *Enough, my friend, of learning, enough!*

This evening instead we tasted "the lesson of love." *(T.B., D.D.)*

July 18: Islam's Many Faces

Just as it is challenging to study Christianity because it has so many faces, it's not easy to study Islam. Dar al-Islam teaches "normative" vs. "descriptive" Islam, that is, the historical origins of the tradition vs. controversial contemporary manifestations. I've really come to appreciate this approach. I now understand that Muslims consider the Qur'an so sacred as the word of God that it cannot be changed, although various Schools of Law interpret it differently. There are also differences from country to country and from region to region within a country. Differences occur between urban and rural areas and, of course, between more and less educated areas.

We have been cautioned against "presentism" or "tempocentrism," that is, evaluating the past from the perspective of today. (Our Spanish friend, Raimon Panikkar, pioneer in interreligious dialogue, calls this same error *"catachronism,"* the opposite of anachronism.)

Fr. Dave and I have just "come home" to Dar al-Islam, which feels more and more like home, after our all too brief day off. We were so tired we hardly talked for twenty-four hours. I slept in till 8 A.M. today and later we did four loads of laundry! Then I did some research on the study project we're sharing with Paul Beverly, who teaches at Eastern Christian High School in North Haledon, New Jersey. (The eighteen of us have divided into groups according to interests.)

We three decided to compare stages of growth in Sufi mysticism (the mysticism, or inner life of Islam) with stages in Christian Mysticism. Most of the people here use the internet extensively, and I long for our Desert Foundation library at home. But I forced myself to look at some Sufi web sites on line and will then fill in with mystical reflections and poems from our wealth of books in Crestone.

I hear the others returning from various outings to the Taos Pueblo, Christ in the Desert monastery, Los Alamos, and hiking at Bandelier National Monument, so I'll close. It's almost time for dinner, and I'm hungry. The food here is excellent: healthy to eat and beautiful to look at, with lots of fresh fruit and vegetables. *(T.B.)*

July 21: Law, Pirates, and the Renaissance

This morning I rode my bike along the Chama River again as the first rays of sunlight awakened the green of cottonwood leaves and the ochre-brown cliffs.

Our first lecture of the day, by Dr. Muhammad Shafi, introduced us to the various schools of jurisprudence that have developed in Muslim cultures. The Qur'an's approximately six thousand verses (*ayahs*) contain about five hundred verses that may be considered "regulations." That means that a lot is left unsaid and unregulated. So, as new situations arise, Muslim scholars team up to decide how to evaluate these new developments, basing their judgments on the Qur'an, the *Hadiths* (reports describing the words, actions, or habits of the prophet Muhammad), analogy, and reason. It was enlightening to learn that these judgments change over time and from country to country.

Dr. Sulayman Nyang then led us through an examination of how relationships within and between western and Muslim cultures have shifted dramatically since the sixteenth century. Portuguese navigators opened new worlds to Europe, which led to the destruction of a previous world of trade and intercultural enrichment among peoples of Africa, the Middle East and India. Vasco da Gama, whom I "met" in grade school as a great hero of the age of discovery, turns out to be more of a pirate than a noble ambassador of "Christian" culture. I remember first receiving this impression from Amitav Ghosh's novel, *In an Antique Land.*

Then came big, sometimes violent changes within western cultures: American, French, and Russian revolutions that changed the understanding of church-state relationships. Whereas these changes have settled into "normalcy" in the West, many Muslim cultures, adjusting to industrialization and new nation-states (usually created by western imperial powers), are in the thick of settling these crucial questions. The revolution in Iran was the mirror image of France: rather than deifying the state and virtually destroying the role of the church, the revolutionaries elevated religious ideology into a political regime.

Finally, we continued our "tour" of the Muslim roots of the European Renaissance with Karima Alavi and saw how, in the midst of European assertion of supremacy over the "benighted" Muslim world, the finest arts and crafts that show up in western art are often products from Syria, Turkey, Iran, Iraq, India, and all the lands along the Silk Route.

We learned that it took centuries for merchants to embrace Arabic numerals. Although using them made accounting much easier, some Europeans suspected that these powerful products of a "heretical" culture were a dangerous kind of "magic." Much of the wisdom and technology we think of as "western" are in fact imports from Muslim cultures. Astrolabes, chemistry, medical and pharmaceutical knowledge, fine fabrics, foods, philosophy—these devices, disciplines, techniques, arts, and crafts owe a debt to Muslim culture.

Of course I loved returning to my favorite period and place: medieval Spain. I never tire of hearing about the great Mosque in Cordoba, the schools of translation in Toledo, and the bittersweet twilight of Muslim culture in Granada. *(D.D.)*

July 22: Jihad, Shi'ites, and Prince among Slaves

It's almost impossible to summarize the clarifying richness of today's classes. First we looked at *jihad* and then terrorism. There is no linguistic linkage between the two. Definitions given in the *Oxford English Dictionary, Webster's Second Edition,* and even *A Dictionary of Modern Written Arabic,* published in 1960, are incorrect. (I know that dictionaries can be wrong because I've seen the prejudicial definitions of "hermit" which clearly do not describe my own eremitical life.)

Jihad means "moral struggle" and differs from *qital,* the word the Qur'an uses for military engagement. We looked at the strict Muslim Rules of Engagement, which made me ashamed of the ways in which the U.S. has gone to war. The Rules against harming non-combatants are especially damning. "Food crops, fruit and shade trees, or any private property cannot be destroyed or appropriated." And most relevant to my own way of life: "Monks, hermits, and all those engaged in religious worship cannot be killed."

We also looked at crucial articles in which official Muslim scholars denounce the horrors of 9/11 and suicide bombing, which is considered murder and "self-killing" and therefore forbidden.

Neither a scholar nor a "rabble-rouser" can declare *jihad,* only a "legitimate executive authority" such as a president, a king, or a sultan, and then only in a state run by Muslims. This means that Osama bin Laden was completely illegitimate in his demands upon other Muslims. The trouble is, naturally, that many Muslims are ignorant of their own orthodox tradition, as so many Christians are ignorant of theirs. (By declaring a caliphate and controlling territory, ISIS later claimed legitimate authority to declare war.)

The second lecture, unfortunately following so close after, was a dense history of the Sunni and Shi'a traditions. I confess that I went almost cross-eyed with all the names—multiple Alis, Muhammads, Hasans and one Husayn; the Shi'ite "Fivers," "Seveners," and "Twelvers"; the Zaydis, the Fatimis, the Nizaris, the Ismailis; the "Rightly Guided Caliphs," the Party of Ali, and rifts within the "Partisans"; and various understandings of the person and power of the "Imam," leading to the twentieth-century inflation of titles such as Ayatollah.

I haven't "unveiled" much of this here, but it's too complicated. What impressed me today is the number of branches in the Shi'ite tradition, varying teachings and beliefs.

The day ended with a showing of a powerful documentary, *Prince among Slaves,* the story of Abdul Rahman Ibrahima Sori, a prince in West Africa who was captured and brought to Mississippi as a slave in the late eighteenth century. This is how Islam first came to America so long ago, although it didn't survive any better than the indigenous cultures of the slaves.

We had two powerful thunderstorms today, and this dry thirsty land is now drenched with rain, and the sunset was glorious as the Call to Prayer rang out through the desert. *(T.B.)*

July 23: Islamic States

This morning Dr. Shafi recounted the history of Muslim understandings of the relationship between Islam and governments. Has there ever been an "Islamic state"? Are there any today? Does the Qur'an talk about this? The answers, respectively, are probably: not since 750, no, and no. With the fall of the Umayyad dynasty in 750, Islam began to differentiate, and governments could eventually be called "Muslim" when the majority of the population became Muslim. But contemporary radicals who may call for a new "universal caliphate" that governs the world according to the teachings of Islam (or politicians who claim that such radicals exist and must be opposed) are not referring to anything that has existed, nor are they referring to anything described or promoted by traditional Muslim teachings.

Dr. Shafi claims that one verse of the Qur'an (4:59) may refer to rulers. Or it may instead refer to other, non-governing authorities in Muslim society. He contends that Muslims are a diverse community spanning many countries and continents, and they establish governments that reflect local customs and cultures. If the local culture does not contradict Islam, then it has more force than some foreign "Muslim" idea about how one ought to govern. I found this a helpful counter to the prevailing propaganda that instills fear by claiming that "the Muslim world" wants to govern the rest of us. "There are no prospects of universal unity on religious doctrine," he concluded, "much less the structure and operation of a state." *(D.D.)*

July 24: Misconceptions

Today was our last day, and another enriching one. First we presented the results of our study projects and take-home lesson plans. The one I liked best was "Islam: Misconceptions and Commonalities." One of the most effective sections listed passages from Jewish, Christian, and Muslim scriptures to "test" whether we would identify the most violent ones as Muslim. If we did, we were wrong.

Two other projects focused on Muslim art and architecture around the world, showing the diversity, and including a virtual tour of Isfahan's Friday Mosque, one of the most famous and magnificent mosques in the world, located south of Tehran.

Project *Sakinah*

The most remarkable project is being done by Dar al-Islam itself. Project *Sakinah*, the Arabic word for "tranquility," is an attempt to wake up the Muslim community to the reality of domestic violence. The project's web site features a "Muslim Wheel of Domestic Violence" developed by Dr. Sharifa Alkahteeb and conveys some of the ways religion can be distorted to justify abuse against women, and not only in Islam.

"Using Male Privilege" is the most enlightening and includes "husband's dominance and inflexibility extolled as Qur'anically mandated requiring obedience in all matters; wife's opinions, aspirations, plans considered as 'Western' and un-Islamic; wife encouraged to fear husband; husband repeats bogus *Hadith* about women bowing to men."

Economic abuse includes "refusing to allow wife to get education or training," and "taking her entire paycheck while Islam allows her to keep it all." We mention these details because of misconceptions about the role of women in Islam. It is crucial to distinguish between what the religion of Islam sanctions and what some Muslims do. And, of course, the same is true for our understanding of all religions.

It's time for our final "banquet" and farewells. I will truly miss all these exceptional people who manifest such intelligence, openness, integrity, and compassion. *(T.B.)*

July 25: Poetry at "Graduation"

Both Fr. Dave and I are adjusting to life away from Dar al Islam and our new friends. While there, we slept in bunk beds in dorms—he with four other men, I with six other women. There was yet another dorm for the married couple who attended. It worked out quite well, and the sense of community was deep.

At the final banquet we all received our certificates of "graduation," having completed fifty-seven (yes, that's right, fifty-seven!) hours of class work. To the tune of "You are my sunshine," we sang to our teachers and the wonderful staff: "You were our teachers, our Islam teachers. You made us study all night and day. When we're alone now, we think of surahs [verses of the Qur'an], and we bend our knees and pray."

Fr. Dave recited a poem he attempted to write in the Sufi style. (The mountains around Dar al Islam are the Sangre de Cristos, the ones which are also in Crestone, and Pedernal is a flat-topped mountain nearby which Georgia O'Keefe loved and frequently painted.)

Heart of Sand

Sometimes on the mesa between the wall
Of Christ's Blood Mountains and the tower of Pedernal;

Sometimes walking the vaulted memory halls
Of the House of Islam I stopped. I heard a call:

Swirling down from a dome it fell on the ear of my heart
Like silent thunder or singing rain. What art

Can sing down storms on song-starved listening land?
Can rain a song to slake a heart of sand?

I wrote a long funny poem trying to summarize the remarkable experience we'd all shared together, taking care to mention each person by name as a tribute full of gratitude to each one. It concludes:

First you were names, then you became faces,
As I go home, on my heart you leave traces.

Tomorrow from here all of us will be gone,
But tonight I must tell you sincerely: "shukran!"*

As I look back on our Abiquiu adventure, the call to prayer deserves special mention. Ali Ellis from Albuquerque is an American convert to Islam. He has a magnificent voice, and his Call to Prayer is the most moving I've heard outside of the Middle East. This call may be my favorite prayer in the world. It always stops me in my tracks and fills me with adoration. I'll miss hearing it several times a day now that I'm home in my Crestone hermitage. *(T.B.)*

*Shukran *is the Arabic word for "thank you."*

18

Three Faiths, One God

Common Ground, Troubled History

David Denny

"Three Faiths, One God: Judaism, Christianity, Islam," a documentary by Gerald Krell and Meyer Odze, presents a challenging and hopeful exploration of the common ground shared by traditions that also share a very troubled history. Jewish, Christian, and Muslim scholars examine our shared scriptural heritage and, without glossing over our differences, offer directions for deeper respect and understanding between our faiths.

Islam's Five Pillars

Viewers meet practitioners of these faiths and witness vignettes of family and ritual life. We learn about common themes in each tradition through examining Islam's five pillars: faith in the oneness of God, pilgrimage, fasting, charity, and prayer. The film provides reassuring evidence of Islam's emphasis on justice and peace as well as Qur'anic teachings on tolerance and respect for non-Muslim believers. Those who wonder about the role of women in Islam will encounter articulate Muslim women who have found personal fulfillment and spiritual depth in their faith.

"Three Faiths" explores how these traditions coexist in the United States, and we observe some remarkable encounters between Jewish, Christian and Muslim Americans. In a Washington D.C. encounter, participants were asked to meet with members of their own faith community to discuss the question: What do I *not* want others to do, say, or think about my tradition? You will want to ponder their presentation to the plenary group and consider this exercise in your own community.

Students from the three faiths who participate in Chicago's Interfaith Youth Corps and tutor other students describe how their prejudices break down as they hear and trust the stories and struggles of their friends from other faiths.

Convivencia

The film looks back on the "*convivencia*" between the three faiths in medieval Spain and deals with contemporary international tragedies, including the murder of *Wall Street Journal* writer Daniel Pearl. Pearl's father appears in a dialogue with Muslim scholar Akbar Ahmed, who describes how the Qur'an condemns the teachings of Osama bin Laden. One of the most moving scenes introduces Umar Ghuman of the Pakistani parliament, who apologizes to Daniel Pearl's father, Judea. One consolation Ghuman can offer is Islam's teaching that a martyr lives forever, and he considers Daniel Pearl a martyr who sought truth, as did Abraham.

Each of our traditions, according to Rabbi Irving Greenburg, has a lot to be modest about, given the ways we have mistreated each other over the centuries. As Christian theologian Krister Stendahl notes, religion is a dangerous thing because it deals with the Absolute. He counsels us to remember that God alone is absolute, and we would do well to resist temptations to claim that the mystery has its exclusive manifestation in my own tradition and that all others must be eliminated.

Symphony of Compassion

We are, in the end, united by our limitations, and we need each other. This is an ecological, rather than monocultural approach to truth. No one is asked to think less of his or her tradition, but rather to bring its beauty and wisdom to the fore in a common effort to live in a symphony of compassion, not a Tower of Babel. Or, as Rabbi Marc Gopin puts it, competition for love leads to unhappiness. Do we really believe in a God who chooses one child as the exclusively favored one?

19

Sisterly Muslims and Brotherly Love

Woman, Man, and God in Modern Islam

David Denny

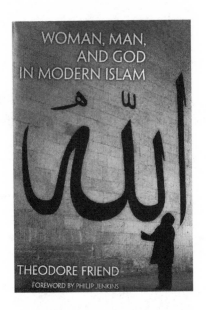

For thirty years I lived at the Spiritual Life Institute, a monastic community that offers hospitality and solitude to retreatants who wish to go into the desert to pray. One of our most fascinating guests was Theodore Friend, a Southeast Asia historian, former president of Swarthmore College, President Emeritus of Eisenhower Fellowships, and a Senior Fellow at the Foreign Policy Research Institute.

Dorie's conversation is always stimulating because he combines a genuine eagerness to hear what his partner has to say and a critical probing that drives me to examine, re-examine, and question the reasonableness of my convictions. He carries this intelligent curiosity through his book, *Woman, Man and God in Modern Islam,* recounting travels and encounters in Indonesia, Pakistan, Saudi Arabia, Iran and Turkey.

Friend travels not as a tourist, but as a pilgrim, friend, and believer deeply concerned with women's well-being, especially in the five countries he visits. He also travels as an historian whose international contacts allow him to meet with government officials, intellectuals, business leaders, activists, artists and theologians.

His ability to place the present plight of women in historical, cultural, and religious context allows him to paint subtle portraits that may shatter some readers' prejudices and stereotypical distortions about Muslim cultures and Muslim women. And, alas, he may confirm some of our greatest concerns about the abuse of women. But his subtle eye is quick to tease out varied sources of abusive behavior rather than automatically condemning "Islam" or "Muhammad."

Friend claims that 1979 was a pivotal year for Islam worldwide. It was the year of the Iranian Revolution, Sunni zealots seized the Grand Mosque in Mecca, Zia al-Haq proclaimed the ghastly Hudood Ordinances in Pakistan, and the Soviet Union invaded Afghanistan. Here in the United States, Jerry Falwell's Moral Majority rose to prominence, reflecting a rising tide of fundamentalism in the Muslim world.

Indonesia

For me, the most hopeful and surprising revelations come in the first chapter on Indonesia, the world's most populous Muslim country. I know much less about Indonesia than about the other four countries, and Friend has long experience in the region. "Islam is all about revelation, about enlightenment, about liberation, about empowerment," according to Indonesia's President Susilo Bambang Yudhoyono. Muslim women throughout the world take this description to heart. Rather than rejecting Islam as inherently and irredeemably misogynist, strong Muslim women's movements seek greater congruence between the Prophet's vision and Muslim practice.

Indonesia's predominantly Sufi Islam and its pre-Muslim

custom of tracing families through both paternal and maternal lines foster a culture averse to demonizing the other: female, Christian, Buddhist, or Hindu. In fact, the 1949 Indonesian constitution deliberately rejected embracing shari'a law out of deference to these other deeply rooted and respected Indonesian communities. At present, and since the nineteen eighties, Indonesian Islam has drifted toward an unprecedented conservatism, due to the worldwide exportation of Wahhabi fundamentalism from Saudi Arabia.

Friend describes the life and work of Wardah Hafidz who, in the present climate, focuses her energies less on combating misogyny and more on poverty and on tsunami recovery in Banda Aceh, where roughly ninety percent of the population died in December 2004. He places the indefatigable Hafidz in the historical context of Malahayati, an Indonesian admiral who commanded the Malacca Strait in the sixteenth century with a force of two thousand women sailors. Hafidz has helped construct over three thousand new homes.

Meutia Hatla is Indonesia's Minister of Women's Empowerment. What kind of country creates such an office? Hatla criticizes male exegetes who miss essential elements in scripture, such as the presence of Mary, who gets more ink in the Qur'an than in the Christian Testament. She insists that the Prophet married for protection of widows, not for desire. She takes a strong stand for Indonesia's history and culture and insists that Arab male standards make no sense there.

She suggests that Arab male insistence on covering women may be a projection of their lustfulness, exacerbated by their carnivorous diet. "Too bad there are no vegetables in the sand," she laments. Friend's more agnostic poet friend Siti Nuraini Jatim takes this playful critique further, with an angry edge, suggesting that "if men are promised seventy-two *houris* [pearl-eyed virginal companions] in paradise, then women deserve seventy-two *toreros* [bull-fighters]!"

Friend gives the final word to Siti Musdah Muliah, the first woman to receive a Ph.D. in Islamic political thinking. She is grounded in the work of Arab philosopher Al-Ghazali, claims the "relativity of muslim law," and insists that "The whole marital law is man-made; none of it is a fax from heaven. Why be afraid? God won't get mad. He's very wise."

Pakistan

If Indonesia's Islam wears a welcoming smile, Pakistan's Islam, since the nineteen eighties, is wary of enemies and is, in some cases, defiantly proud of the "Muslim bomb" produced by physicist A.Q. Khan and detonated in 1998. The nuclear program is a stand against India and a fulfillment of Zulfikar Ali Bhutto's assertion that Pakistanis would eat grass, but they would have their bomb. After all, he said, we have Christian, Jewish, Hindu and communist bombs.

Friend's statistics about Pakistani poverty paint a dire portrait. Sixty-six percent of the population lives on less than two dollars a day. Literacy is less than fifty percent, and much lower for women. Desperate families send their boys to one of approximately thirteen thousand madrasas, private Islamic schools that attempt to make up for the lack of public schools. They also promote anti-Western, puritanical (but not usually violent) Islam.

Women such as Shahnaz Wazir Ali promote schools for girls and women's rights to own land, have access to credit, and earn the financial means to help their children.

As for violence against women, Friend notes that it is not simply attitudinal or subtle. Expressions include "wife-beating, bride-burning, acid-throwing, rape, and murder." In four months in 2003, 211 women were reported killed by kin. Most victims are between sixteen and twenty-five years old, married, and poor. Dowry disputes, husbands' cruelty, suspicion of infidelity, forced sex, and tribal friction are main contributors. Probably only ten percent of survivors testify in court.

I will not summarize the story of rape victim Mukhtaran Bibi here. It is important to know her name, to take the time to learn her story, and to stand in awe of her courage in fighting for the rights of her neighbors and her commitment to educating children.

Saudi Arabia

The first word that comes to mind as I recall Friend's descriptions of Saudi Arabia is "surreal." The contrast with the grinding poverty of Pakistan boggles the mind. Saudi wealth built the world's second-tallest building, the Royal Mecca Clock Tower that looms over the Kaaba. Saudi-Wahhabi Islamic authorities ban women from driving. Friend points out that, different as they are, both Saudi Arabia and Iran are skeptical of "civil society," and claim to represent model Islamic states. Their leaders believe that a proper society is governed from above, by God and God's human representatives.

Friend gives some history of the Wahhabi movement that struck an alliance with the house of Saud in the eighteenth century. He also narrates a concise history of twentieth-century imperialism, the fall of the Ottoman Empire, and the arrival of Aramco in 1933. Friend writes that the British lost the initial bid to drill for oil in Arabia because they also wished to influence Arabian culture. America just wanted oil.

Three-quarters of the Saudi cabinet were educated in the United States, and many educated technocrats have smart plans for the future. But Friend wonders if the culture and religion will cooperate. Saudi women are more educated than the men and ninety percent believe they have the right to choose their husbands. But the religion-state emphasizes obedience and the right of old men to marry child brides. No Muslim woman may marry a Christian, nor can she ever be alone with a man who is not a relative.

But Friend was the first male ever to tour the women's college in Jeddah. Founded in 1999, the curriculum includes business, management and soon, engineering. The students wear *abayas*, robes with hoods or scarves. Friend notes that no foreigner may dress as a Saudi. Americans, for example, may earn huge salaries, but they are not allowed to assimilate.

Friend interviewed Madeha al-Ajroush, a psychotherapist and photographer who took part in the "drivers" protest in 1990. Forty-seven women drove cars, were jailed briefly, and persecuted thereafter. The United States was not eager for this story to be broadcast because it reflects badly on our ally. Madeha suggests that women are treated as sex objects in both Saudi and American cultures. They are publicly promoted as such in the United States, whereas they are closeted in Saudi Arabia. But many of the "drivers" have started NGOs, become university professors, and founded charities such as Mothers of Riyadh, which offers aid for the poor, and Family Safety, an organization against domestic violence.

The most surrealistic image in Friend's account takes place after his visit with Prince Nayef bin Sultan bin Fawwaz Al-Sha'lan. Prince Nayef earned degrees in international relations at Princeton and engineering in Miami. He discussed Christianity with Friend, noting its scriptural contradictions, impervious to Friend's elegant exegesis, and leaving Friend with the impression that the Prince values clarity over mystery, with the Qur'an offering perfect clarity.

Upon returning to the United States, Friend conducted more research on his royal host and discovered that in 2007, a French court found Prince Nayef guilty of smuggling cocaine on his Boeing 727. He continues, Friend notes, to study the Abrahamic religions.

Iran

Thirty years after Iran's revolution, the 2009 elections provided an opportunity to challenge the "sacred system" instituted by Ayatollah Khomeini. Democratic forces questioned the establishment. The wife of the main opposition candidate,

Mir-Hossein Moussavi, campaigned with her husband and promised that women would take cabinet posts in her husband's government. But after their loss, an estimated eighteen thousand protestors were arrested.

Friend's 2005 visit to Iran helped him to understand the turmoil of 2009. He gives a clear account of the history that has led to some Iranians' resistance to democracy. Great Britain and the United States overthrew Prime Minister Muhammad Mossadegh in 1953, in part because he did not see the justice of British Petroleum's taking seven-eighths of Iran's oil revenue. This, coupled with the later temporary United States asylum for the deposed and ailing Shah and support for Saddam Hussein's use of chemical weapons against Iran, provoked strong anti-American passions.

Before embarking on a dangerous pilgrimage, Friend met publisher Makan Zahrai, who noted that more books are published in Iran than in the entire Arab world. By emphasizing their ancient non-Arab culture and a reading public, Iranians attempt to explain how they are different from their Sunni Arab neighbors. Seventy percent of the population is under thirty, and sixty-three percent of college students are women.

But in spring of 2000, eighteen reformist journals were closed in one day. Daryush Shayegan, professor of comparative philosophy and theology, complains that the Revolution expelled anyone with governing experience and elevated priests who claim to know a lot about life in the seventh century and about heaven, but make the worst possible governors.

In such an environment, women do not do well. No female candidates were approved in 2005 elections. Iran has a movie industry, although many theaters were burned during the Revolution. Actress Tamineh "Bati" Milani has produced nine feature-length films dealing with middle class Iranian women. In response to her 2001 film "Hidden Half," she earned four death penalties. She was spared only because she was a friend of then-president Khatemi who, after a perplexing search, finally found her in the terrifying Evin Prison and freed her.

Iran is also the home of the world's first Muslim woman recipient of the Nobel Peace Prize: Shirin Ebadi. A judge before the Revolution, she was demoted and later left Iran. She continues to fight for human rights in Iran.

Friend's account of Iran includes some of his most personal reflections. His wife had recently died, and his daughter was about to undergo a liver transplant. Against the advice of his friends, he determined to visit Mashhad, the only shrine of a Shi'ite imam in Iran, a place few non-Shi'ites ever see. He wanted to make a pilgrimage and pray for his family.

Mashhad is five hundred miles east of Tehran, along the Silk Road. Its shrine is larger than Vatican City. The gracious scholar Farhad Rahimi agrees to accompany Friend on his pilgrimage. Friend clings to Rahimi's shirt tail as they make their way through a teeming crowd of weeping pilgrims determined to toss offerings of money, mementos and flowers through the shrine's golden lattice.

Once out of the crowd, Friend weeps with Rahimi for his mother, his wife Elizabeth, and his daughter as his fears, longings and deepest concerns overwhelm him. Rahimi proclaims this a miracle. (Friend's daughter Timmie recovered from her transplant and two years later bore a child.)

Friend's final reflections on Iran concern the uniqueness of Shi'ite messianism, with its hope for the coming of the Mahdi, who will usher in the End Time. Shi'ism was born out of the martyrdom of the Prophet's grandson, Ali, and this combination of exalted martyrdom and apocalypticism make Iran the most volatile of the five countries Friend visited.

Turkey

Friend concludes his journey in Turkey, the westernmost of his destinations. Touching Europe in its fabled Istanbul, once known as Constantinople, Turkey has moved from being the seat of the Ottoman Empire and the caliphate to being the most secular of the five countries Friend visits. Friend briefly examines the life of Mustapha Kemal, "Ataturk," father of modern Turkey.

As the Ottoman Empire fell and the Allies sliced up its territory after World War I, war hero Ataturk rose to power and swiftly transformed his nation. He abolished the sultanate and caliphate, promoted western music and dance, closed Sufi lodges and shrines, introduced the "Christian" calendar and drew on European precedents for new civil, penal and business codes. He instituted the Roman alphabet, discouraged Persian and Arabic names, and promoted mass education. A charismatic leader with a military background, the Turkish military became his staunch enforcer of secularization.

This energetic revolution from the top enabled women to vote in local elections in 1930, and by 1935, eighteen women were members of parliament. Ataturk banned religious clothing outside mosques and formal religious ceremonies. In his fifteen years in power, literacy doubled, as did per capita income.

This prodigious secular thrust continued into the later twentieth century, and Friend offers us a fascinating look at Turkish development through his long friendship with former prime minister and President Süleyman Demirel. Having visited the United States in the fifties, Demirel was amazed at what Americans had accomplished and went home to pour his energies into building dams, highways, schools, and encouraging mass communication technology.

But with the international rise of Muslim anti-western movements, Islamists emerged as a political force in Turkey. They won elections in 1995, but the military forced them from power in 1997. In 2002, the current president, Islamist Recep Tayyip Erdogan, won office, and Turkey is working out a new dynamic in the balance of power. It includes not only the "Kemalist" secularists and the Islamists, but new political parties, vocal social critics, and a more independent judiciary. Where do women fit in this new dynamic? Even before Ataturk's reforms, Muslim scholar Fatma Aliya challenged a powerful sheikh's contention that the Qur'an and the Prophet commanded all men to take four wives. In the early twentieth century, painter and opera star Semiha Berksoy became an international celebrity. But women's illiteracy today is four times higher than men's.

Friend interviews Turkish women who choose to cover their hair and others who do not. Fatma Benli earned a law degree in 1995, but she cannot complete her masters because she wears a turban. The president's wife and other high officials' wives who do not cover their hair simply do not appear in public. The penal code was revised in 2004, acknowledging women's rights and legislating against rape in marriage and sexual harassment.

Friend describes the work of lawyer Vildan Yirmibeşoğlu, who moved to southeastern Turkey in 1984 and was startled by the lack of women in public places. She began to meet with women and learn about violence against them. In 1998 Vildan returned to Istanbul and helped pass new laws protecting women. The violence, she finds, is not a result of Muslim teachings, but of the failure of Islam to eradicate pre-Muslim practices.

Friend departs from the secular concerns of contemporary Turkish politics to venture inland to medieval Sufi poet Jalaluddin Rumi's city of Konya. There he encounters traditional Sufi hospitality and describes being spellbound by the celebration of a Sufi dance meditation attended by a thousand people. Friend notes that Ataturk would be surprised by the enduring presence of Islam in today's Turkey.

He concludes that while the tension between the secular-military faction and the Islamists may threaten stability, it may also pave the way for a richer pluralism that is not simply bipolar.

Power, Culture, and Equality

Friend reflects on each of the five countries he visited and on the need for a fundamental "poise," a power of cohesion necessary to help preserve stability in the midst of crisis, deprivation or doubt. He finds that Turkey and Indonesia seem to possess more of this poise than Pakistan, Saudi Arabia or Iran.

In his final chapter, he reflects on his personal encounters, on the latest data on human rights and women's rights in the countries he visited, on troubling obstacles to women's flourishing, and his hopes for women and Islam.

Pakistan's chronic anarchy does not bode well for women. In Saudi Arabia, women are still considered "chattel" by many men. No one there is paid to protect women, but many draw pay for upholding propriety and punishing women. Yet it appears that many Saudi citizens believe a woman has a right to choose her spouse and agree that a woman can initiate a divorce.

Friend makes it clear that honor killings are neither Muslim nor Arab. They occur in non-Arab countries and are rare or non-existent in Muslim Indonesia and Malaysia. As for Iran, it ranks low in the Global Gender Gap Index, but women's status is discussable and women's achievements are significant, such as Shirin Ebadi's Nobel Prize for Peace. Some women vote. But the Supreme Leader's power to punish and monitor the people equals that of the shahs.

Turkey, with its traditional state suspicion of Islam and especially Sufis, its patriarchal traditions, and resurgent Muslim conservatism leaves women there less safe and secure than in Indonesia. On the one hand, they are caught in the middle of these forces, and on the other hand, they may be part of a rising critical social voice that may help assure a healthier pluralism.

Obstacles to Progress

Two strict obstacles to progress are what Friend calls "hypertextualism," a claim to complete infallible understanding of the Qur'an, and "culturalism," imprisonment of the Qur'an in a limited cultural context. Both these positions exclude the possibility of true conversation within and between religions and cultures.

Friend suggests that using religion to suppress women's rights is as anachronistic as "Christian" justifications for slavery. He astutely notes that men suffer greatly when they possess unjust power over women and miss the depth and beauty of mutuality and complementarity. Friend notes that feminists of the Muslim South are more at home with religion than some of their North Atlantic counterparts. Rather than making resistance and rejection their mode of operation,

> *they make friendly propositions... They compare and they cross religious boundaries. They delight in heresy and humor. They offer insight, drive, creativity, and spiritual witness. They invite men to stop castrating each other with radical fundamentalisms. Because they are rooted in the underground, they can offer complementary dialogue with men, and creative polylogue among cultures and religions.*

Friend is unwilling to exonerate religions from charges of misogyny and atrocity. Nor is he willing to reject religion. "Insofar as either 'Allah' or 'God' invokes an Abrahamic god of live sacrifice and vengeance, I would that we shun such altars. Thunder-and-slaughter gods must give way to light and mercy and compassionate justice. Not because anger is ungodly, but because murder is unholy."

Five Feminine Needs

Friend sums up five needs for which heroic Muslim women fight: a strong sense of identity as human with a right to flourish; the right to choose education and resist suffocation; the need to break stereotypes and express individuality that is often manifest in the arts; the need to have women's equality reflected in enforced laws that demonstrate a creative respect for tribal and religious tradition while weeding out misogynist anachronisms and injustices. Fifth, women need variety and the acceptance of "alterity," so that, for example, they may cover their heads or not, without suffering discrimination.

In the end, Friend expresses hope not in a "moderate" Islam, a term he finds insulting, but rather an "open" Islam that revives the liberating power that undermined caste and racist systems in its early years and expanded women's rights. An open Islam would spread its tent to include women as equals and rediscover the glory of mystics such as Rumi and Hafez.

Arab Uprisings

As Friend's book was at press, great shifts erupted in North Africa and the Middle East, prompting his epilogue dealing with what he calls the "Arab Uprisings," rather than the "Arab Spring." It is too soon to know if these turbulent outbursts predict a true "springtime." If a true spring comes to Tunisia or Syria, it may be autumn in Egypt or Iran.

Friend's historical perspective is especially interesting here. He reexamines fourteenth-century historian Ibn Khaldun's understanding of the rise and fall of civilizations. Ibn Khaldun observed two fundamental movements in human development: Bedouin and urban life. He contended that Bedouin family bonds were the strongest unifying force in society. These bonds weaken as nomads settle in cities.

Urban dwellers no longer know how to live in small bands, moving with the seasons, according to availability of food and water. They relinquish their arms and hire princes and police to protect them. Inevitably, corruption sets in, and the city is ripe for raiding by Bedouins who may be savage, but also possess virtues forgotten by urban dwellers, including fierce family bonds and a primal connection with nature.

Friend suggests that Ibn Khaldun could not have imagined the rise of what we now call civil society and democracy. The Muslim world, insofar as it has clung to this bipolar understanding that there are only two classes, the governors and the governed, and two cultures, desert nomads and urban dwellers, is ill-equipped to deal with a democratic dynamic.

I am grateful to my friend and brother, Theodore Friend, for taking us far deeper than headlines and sharing the "heartlines" opened between him and his Muslim sisters.

Dear Fr. Dave: What I most deeply appreciate about your long and thoughtful reflection on my book is its authoritative coping with the full range of my thinking. I was afraid nobody would pick up what I say about the five dimensions of [Muslim] women's future fulfillment—identity, choice, individuality, equality, and variety. You have it all, nuanced and in your own language. The epilogue on the Arab uprisings was done at the request of my publisher, to which I acceded with misgiving about its quickly becoming outdated. But you handle that segment nicely, with your own sensibilities. I respect your ways of picking up my emphases in each of the country chapters. And you are right to see that Indonesia presented itself to me as the opening chapter, because so much of what I wished to say had been said so well by Indonesians. You make me happy to have put seven years into the work.

Theodore Friend
Author of Woman, Man, and God in Modern Islam

20
Are Muslims a Threat to Us?

Listening to John Esposito

David Denny

The Desert Foundation has been concerned about the rise of Islamophobia in the United States and Europe, especially since the 9/11 terrorist attacks and the 11/9 election. In 2014, I heard a news report on a Tennessee town in which a young Muslim expressed her fear and sorrow after an attack on her mosque. I heard attendees applaud and cheer the attack rather than the woman's courage for speaking up. "Hundreds of activists heckled a United States Attorney who was making a speech on hate crimes," NPR reported, "and cheered as Muslims described the firebombing of a nearby mosque."

In response to a painful experience of anti-Muslim rhetoric in nearby Alamosa, Colorado, several local organizations sponsored a lecture by John Esposito, a world authority on Islam.

Humor and Smarts

Dr. Esposito is Founding Director of the Prince Alwaleed Bin Talal Center for Muslim-Christian Understanding at Georgetown University's School of Foreign Service. He has served as a consultant for the United States Department of State and for other governments and corporations in Europe and Asia. He has also been Vice Chair of the World Economic Forum's Council of 100 Leaders. In 2013 he was President of the American Academy of Religion.

Given his academic credentials and my own prejudices, I was prepared for the possibility of a calm-to-boring lecture full of stats and short on brio. Wrong. Esposito grew up in an Italian-Catholic working class family in Brooklyn and has the humor and smarts to match. Tessa and I had heard he spent ten years in a monastery. We met him before the talk and asked about it. He said he spent a decade, from age fourteen–twenty-four, in a Franciscan community, and his mom loved it because it increased his chances of being a virgin when he married. Esposito's light heart allows him to present troubling material in a spirit of hope.

Stereotypes and Generalizations

Early in his talk he reminded us that many Americans' first exposure to Islam came with the 1979 Iran hostage crisis, portrayed in the movie *Argo*. He noted that television news anchor Tom Brokaw felt it necessary to inform us that Islam is a religion founded by a prophet, Muhammad, with a scripture called the Qur'an. Esposito suggested that something is wrong when a journalist must explain that to a well-educated population. How is it that we know so little about a tradition that has been with us since the seventh century and has had a great influence on western philosophy, science, and arts? How is it that we know so little about our 1.6 billion Muslim neighbors?

Esposito confirmed that stereotypes are powerful and reminded us of how easy it is to generalize about groups of people based on very limited contact. For example, if I am a struggling Polish immigrant in the United States and an Irish worker gets the job I want, I may be tempted to believe that the Irish are out to impoverish or crush the Poles. So when we found out that the handful of men who destroyed the World Trade Center were Muslims, it was too easy to see them simply as Muslims, not as Saudi citizens or members of an extremist group that claims to be Muslim while violating fundamental Muslim teachings.

Esposito also questioned American law enforcement's reaction to the horror of 9/11. We subjected more than five thousand Arab and Muslim foreign nationals within the United States to preventive detention—not one of whom stands convicted of a terrorist offense. In a note of dark humor, Esposito wondered why we do not round up an equivalent number of Italian Americans in order to combat the mafia.

If It Bleeds, It Leads

"If it bleeds, it leads," we used to say about newspaper headlines. Esposito noted the difference in media references to Muslims over the years. In 2001, in 975,000 media references to Islam, two percent of the articles referred to extremism and 0.1 percent referred to mainstream Islam. In 2011, twenty-eight percent referred to extremism while references to mainstream Islam remained at 0.1 percent. These statistics seem incredible.

I remember the controversy over the "Ground-Zero Mosque" in New York City. As Esposito noted, the project is neither a mosque, although it includes a prayer space, nor is it at Ground Zero. It is a community center based on a Jewish model in Manhattan's Upper West Side. New Yorkers seemed relatively open to it until social media sparked a backlash against a "monument to terrorism."

Esposito suggests that this is similar to referring to St. Patrick's Cathedral as a monument to pedophilia. Terrorism and pedophilia are grave blights, to be taken seriously and resisted vigorously, but few Christians are ready to disband their churches as a result of behavior disorders and criminal activity in some of our ministers.

Some politicians and pundits have raised the question of whether Muslims can be loyal Americans. Roman Catholics have also faced this challenge. Here in Colorado, shortly after the founding of Holy Cross Abbey in Cañon City in 1924, the Ku Klux Klan burned crosses in five of the city's main intersections, hoping to intimidate local Catholics.

We may think that few Americans wish to be known as Klan-like, yet seven major philanthropic organizations have donated over forty million dollars to anti-Muslim causes, such as the demonstrations against the Muslim center in New York. The Council on American-Islamic Relations (CAIR) estimates that an inner core of thirty-seven American anti-Muslim groups received more than 119 million dollars between 2008 and 2011.

Anti-Muslim Prejudice

Financial support for anti-Muslim prejudice helps account for the majority of Americans who have a negative attitude toward Islam and Muslims. And yet American Muslims are second only to Jews in education. Forty percent have college degrees, compared to twenty-nine percent of Americans. Thomas Jefferson insisted that education is essential for the health of democracy.

Esposito points out that religion has a shadow side. We know how easily violence may be "justified" by scriptural references. The Qur'an and the life of Muhammad attest to the possibility of defending oneself and one's community against aggression. But few Jews and Christians are ready to defend the "ban" practiced in the book of Numbers or 1 Samuel that sounds to us like genocide.

Just as we are prone to generalize too easily from limited exposure to someone "other," we are also prone to present the ideals of our own tradition as normative ("Christianity is a peaceful religion.") while presenting the worst of another tradition as normative ("Muslims are terrorists."). Even though the Gospels advocate peace and Jesus blesses peacemakers, it did not take long for Christianity to become an agent of mass violence, first under Roman Emperor Constantine and later during the Crusades.

My own travels in Muslim countries, from Afghanistan to Tunisia, Egypt, and Jordan, have always been filled with hospitality and good will. I know this is not the case for everyone, and I also respect Esposito's insight that one ought not to generalize, for good or ill, from limited experience. But the statistics Esposito cites certainly affirm his experience and mine: Muslims, here in America or abroad, continue the practice of hospitality that is a hallmark of Muslim tradition.

21
The Unifying Element

Hatred or Peace?

David Denny

A friend asked me to comment on chaos and destruction in the Middle East. The Syrian civil war, Iraq's struggle with ISIS, and continuing violence in Israel/Palestine have been devastating. Shootings in San Bernardino in 2015 and months later in Orlando raised anew the question of whether Islam is inherently violent and whether American Muslims can be trusted. "Breaking news" reports and immediate reactions flared as President Obama's tenure wound down and primary campaigns heated up.

We need time for careful, prayerful thought and reflection, for education and respect between communities. So my friend's question about violence in the Middle East led me to reflect on violence in our own culture and in human nature.

Columnist Andrew Sullivan represents the careful, if not prayerful thought, that can illuminate this Dark Age. In a *New York* magazine article, he reflects on Plato's critique of democracy and suggests that current trends in the United States, including the explosion of social media, have undermined thoughtfulness, replacing it with "what [America's] Founders feared about democratic culture: feeling, emotion, and narcissism, rather than reason, empiricism, and public-spiritedness." Hatred, according to American writer Eric Hoffer, is "the most accessible and comprehensive of all unifying elements."

Personal Transformation

These dark waters deserve more exploration. But here are two simple assumptions I have adopted. *First*, I do not listen to anyone who generalizes about a religion. As we know, practicing Christianity in the United States may be very different than in India or Colombia. And within these countries,

Christianity takes many forms. The same for Islam. So I try not to pay attention to folks who assert that Islam is "inherently violent" unless they are ready to say the same about Christianity, Judaism, and human nature and are willing to look for a cure, not through violent elimination of the "infidel," but by personal transformation and the search for non-violent teachings that lie at the heart of these "violent" traditions.

As many historians note, Christianity and Islam make "universal" claims that have been wedded to political imperialism. We need to acknowledge this dark legacy. Iranian-American author, commentator and religious scholar Reza Aslan reminded CNN reporters in 2014 that religions don't necessarily promote peace or violence. Violent members of these religions promote violence, as peaceful members promote peace. Even some Burmese Buddhists have perpetrated violence against Muslims and Christians in Myanmar.

The Great Divide

Second, I believe that conflicts between Abrahamic populations are rarely "religious." They are *human*, including political and economic. People who suffer historic injustices and are oppressed not only by poverty but by political corruption or cultural and religious prejudice, are often driven to extreme and violent behavior. And then we tend to blame them.

What breaks my heart is that new oppressors arise who offer huge amounts of money and arms to "empower" these desperate populations. "The great divide," wrote Nicholas Kristof in the *New York Times*, "is not between faiths, but one between intolerant zealots of any tradition and the large numbers of decent, peaceful believers likewise found in each tradition."

We surely need to go much deeper in order to understand the dynamics of "religious" violence, and my two assumptions are themselves debatable generalizations. But they're not bad as starting points toward arriving at a "unifying element" more peaceful and truthful than hatred.

22
Cross and Crescent

George Dardess, David Denny, George Leonard,
and Jamal Rahman in Conversation

Fr. David Denny Begins

*George Leonard of Long Beach, Mississippi wrote a thoughtful
letter raising questions about Islam that came up in his neighborhood church's discussion group. Rather than answering him
directly, I invited two friends to join the conversation: Roman
Catholic Deacon George Dardess and Imam Jamal Rahman.
George has worked and prayed with the Muslim community
in Rochester, New York for years. He is the author of* Meeting
Islam: A Guide for Christians. *Jamal Rahman resides in Seattle and often speaks about possibilities for peace between the
Abrahamic traditions. His book,* The Fragrance of Faith, *is a
wonderful introduction to the warm, wise path he walks, inherited from his Bangladeshi ancestors.*

Dr. George Leonard Writes

Fr. Dave, our neighborhood church discussion group has
been struggling with Islam. Some say it is a Religion of Peace,
and others call it a Religion of War and Violence. We guestimate
that only about ten percent of Muslims are radical extremists,
but what about the other ninety percent?

Some quote the violence in the Qur'an, and the fact that
even Muhammad, considered by himself and his followers to be
the greatest of all prophets, led armies of plunder and is said to
have murdered almost thousands with his own hands. Yet much
of the Qur'an decries violence, and Muhammad was on other
days a very gentle and peaceful and loving man.

Why aren't the moderate Muslims more vocal? We
understand that Muhammad lived in a time and culture of
violence, and that Christianity had its times of extreme violence
also, as in the Crusades. And that the Old Testament was full of

violence. But that doesn't seem to explain it all. At the end of the day, Jesus was a peaceful loving man, and true Christianity obviously a religion of Peace and Love. How do you see it?

Deacon George Dardess Responds

Dr. Leonard, Fr. Dave has passed your thoughtful letter on to me and asked me to respond. I'm glad to do so, and hope very much I can help.

First of all, I'm pleased that you and your church discussion group have been "struggling with Islam." I'm pleased, because by doing so, you're showing you refuse to settle for the instant opinions that come to us on this and every other matter through the major media. You've instead chosen to "struggle with Islam" in the context of prayer and honest soul-searching reflection. This is grace-filled and will bear fruit, if you can keep at it.

The temptation is to yield to what we're told about Islam and Muslims by the usual news outlets. Those outlets are extremely unreliable about Islam as about so much else that concerns our common interests. Sensationalism and the "bottom line" tend to govern the media's decisions about what goes out over the airwaves and how it is presented.

Muslims Speak Out

It is simply not true that "moderate" Muslims are "not vocal." The problem is that they cannot get a hearing in the major media. Part of the problem is because there is no central figure in Islam, like the Pope, who can presume to speak for all or at least a great number of the faithful. But even when "moderate" Muslims do gather to write and issue important documents emphasizing the common prophetic values all members of the Abrahamic religions share— love of God and love of neighbor— they are barely mentioned in our media.

I doubt very much that the document "A Common Word between Us and You," published by the Kingdom of Jordan and signed by over a hundred influential Muslim clerics, took up much or any space at all in your newspapers or any time on your TV broadcasts. Yet it is a significant statement by the "moderate Muslims" that we so often hear "are not speaking out." If your church group has not yet seen this letter, please urge them to do so and visit the various other links offered at www.acommonword.com.

Islamica and *Horizons*

Other websites you should investigate to get the flavor of "moderate Muslims" in the United States are for two leading Muslim magazines, *Islamica* and *Horizons,* the magazine of the Islamic Society of North America, or ISNA. Visiting these sites will quickly introduce you to an obscured world of "moderate Muslims" doing their best to be good citizens in a country that is growing increasingly hostile to them.

You say that "true Christianity is obviously a religion of Peace and Love." I couldn't agree more. Yet you and I both have to admit that over the course of the centuries, this "true Christianity" has been sadly betrayed by those acting violently in her name. As a Roman Catholic, I'm ashamed to have to point out my own denomination's preaching of Holy War to initiate the Crusades. I could give many other examples of similar betrayals of Christ's teachings by his self-proclaimed followers, and not just in the dim past either.

I mention these sins not to denigrate Christianity. My point is that both the past and the present contain many sad instances not only of Muslims betraying the foundational teachings of their religion, but of Christians doing likewise. We are all sinners. My hope for the future is that, as one people under God, Christians and Muslims can work together to fulfill our common mandate to Peace and Love.

Imam Jamal Rahman Responds

Dr. Leonard, many thanks for your interest in interfaith dialogue. In the Qur'an, the Prophet Muhammad is the "Seal of the Prophets." This means that there will be no more Prophets of Revelation till the Day of Judgment.

The Holy Book repeatedly warns that no Muslim, including the Prophet Muhammad himself, should discriminate between the Prophets. In a telling verse, God tells the Prophet Muhammad: "There is nothing revealed to you that has not been revealed to other Apostles" (41:43). It is against the spirit of the Qur'an for a Muslim or non-Muslim to boast that the Prophet Muhammad is the greatest of all Prophets.

Muhammad

I hope you will not misunderstand me when I tell you that every Muslim will reject your remarks about the Prophet Muhammad [murdering "almost thousands" of non-Muslims with his own hands, etc.] as historical untruth, propaganda and fabrication. Over the centuries, many scholars, Muslim and non-Muslim, have pointed out that the Prophet's detractors, from the seventh century to the present time, have systematically and deliberately spread false rumors about him, fearful and frustrated that an "upstart" from nowhere burst upon the Arabian landscape, successfully challenged the corruption of the religious institutions of his time, and attracted an extraordinary number of followers. I recommend the work of contemporary scholar Reuven Firestone, who has researched this issue.

I am not saying that Muslims are above resorting to tactics of slander and character assassination. The lower self, when motivated by fear or arrogance, whether Muslim or Christian, does not behave with honor. But there is a lopsidedness here that I, as a Muslim, urgently need to point out.

Some Christians who are upset by Islamic extremists might unabashedly criticize and castigate the Prophet Muhammad, often in vile terms. But no Muslim, no matter how angry he or she is about the behavior of Christians, will ever utter one word against Jesus, who is deeply revered in Islam as a Prophet and called "Spirit of God" in the Qur'an. No Muslim will ever mention Jesus or any Prophet without uttering in the same breath, "Peace and Greetings be upon him."

The lack of awareness about the authentic life and ministry of the Prophet Muhammad in the West is tragic and, in my opinion, is both the cause and effect of bias and prejudice. I recommend reading *A Prophet for our Times* by Karen Armstrong. How many non-Muslims know that the Prophet Muhammad was a profound mystic, who from a tender age meditated regularly in the majestic silence of the Meccan caves, sometimes for forty days and nights? The Qur'an has its roots in the womb of silence when the Prophet experienced an epiphany called the "Night of Power."

How many know the historical truth that when delegations of Jews and Christians visited the Prophet in the seventh century, he always requested them to do the Shabbat and Sunday Service in the Mosque, for "it is a place simply consecrated to God?" How many know that two of the Prophet's wives were Jews and one was a Christian?

People of the Book

How many know that the phrase, "People of the Book," appears often in the Qur'an and that the word "Book" is always in the singular, suggesting that the Qur'an is a third installment of the same Book? In a remarkable revelation, the Qur'an says:

We believe in God
And what has been sent down to us
What has been revealed to Abraham and Ishmael
And Isaac and Jacob and their offspring
And what was given to Moses and Jesus
And all other Prophets by the Creator
And we make no distinction between them.
(Qur'an 2:136)

The Qur'an does have difficult and awkward verses whose meaning depends on the interpreter's state of consciousness and intention. In the imagery of the Islamic mystic Rumi, both bee and wasp drink from the same flower, but one produces nectar and the other a sting.

Some verses, if read literally and in historical isolation, lend themselves to exploitation. For example, the Qur'an tells us, "Take not the Jews and Christians for your friends and protectors. They are friends and protectors to each other" (Qur'an 5:51). Without knowing the historical context of this verse, one could certainly read it as a condemnation of Jews and Christians, but scholars agree that this verse refers to a specific historical incident and is certainly not a universal condemnation.

Another verse in the same chapter affirms the basic goodness of other believers: "Those who believe, those who follow the Jewish scriptures, the Christians, the Sabians, and any who believe in God and the Final Day and do good, all shall have their reward with their Sustainer and they will not come to fear and grief" (Qur'an 5:69).

Who Speaks for Islam?

Regarding violence and extremism, *Who Speaks for Islam? What a Billion Muslims Really Think*, by Dalia Mogahed and John Esposito, is critical for our times. It summarizes a mammoth and unprecedented Gallup Poll study (2001 to 2007) of a sample representing more than ninety percent of the world's 1.3 billion Muslims in fifty-seven countries. It allows data to lead the discourse.

A major insight is that militant theology is created not by Islamic principles but by political radicalization. The majority of Muslims believe that the "ruthless" United States government is neither serious nor sincere about fostering democracy in Muslim countries and that western policy is rooted in disrespect for Islam and a desire for economic and political domination. The war on Islamic terrorism is viewed as a war on Islam. Contrary to popular belief, the data says that the politically radicalized, even more than the moderate, are eager to foster governmental democracy in Muslim countries.

We live in difficult times. Many Christian and Muslim hearts are clenched because of fear, anger, distrust and suspicion. The Qur'an explains, "It's not that their eyes have become blind, but their hearts" (Qur'an: 22:46).

How can we open hearts? How can we restore love and harmony to a relationship that has been hurt and damaged? Force will only cause more clenching. Reason will help a little, but it is not enough. Only what comes from the heart can open another heart.

A problem cannot be solved at the level of the problem. We have to rise above it. We have to become more authentic and more evolved. We have to open our hearts. From that spaciousness will emerge loving and creative solutions.

Whose Religion is Better?

We need to take to heart Mahatma Gandhi's plea that if a religious extremist commits violence, please do not criticize that person's religion. Rather, point out to this person verses and insights of beauty and wisdom from the person's own tradition. Help this person become a better Muslim, Christian, Jew or Hindu. This, Gandhi explained, is the way to peace in a pluralistic society.

Spiritual teachers from all traditions have pointed out that if someone says, "My religion is better than yours," this is not religion speaking, but one's untamed ego. It is wise to meditate on Alexsander Solzhenitsyn's profound insight:

If it were all so simple! If only there were evil people somewhere insidiously committing evil deeds, and it were necessary only to separate them from the rest of us and destroy them. But the line dividing good and evil cuts through the heart of every human being. And who is willing to destroy a piece of his own heart?

The Qur'an says, "Repel evil with something better so that

your enemy becomes your bosom friend" (Qur'an: 41:34). In another passage, the Holy Book says that God created diversity so that "we might get to know one another" (Qur'an: 49:13). Of course we have to protect ourselves, but we also have to open our hearts and get to know the other on a personal level, as children of God, and without any agenda, whether the person is a Christian or Muslim extremist.

God is forcing us to go beyond our conditioned biases, excuses and patterns. Our Creator is telling us that if we have the time and energy to engage the other in conflict and hatred, we indeed have the time and energy to engage in dialogue, compassionate listening, higher awareness and right action. "God, the Lord of Grace unbounded" (Qur'an 2:105) will help us in our sincere endeavors.

23
Do All Lives Have Equal Value?

Christians Facing Persecution

David Denny

"**W**orry" seems too shallow a word for what I felt after the 2015 Charlie Hebdo Paris shootings, ISIS depredations, and anti-Islam reactions. Conversation with Jamal Rahman, a wise, kind, radiant Muslim friend, helped me remain hopeful about a more respectful attitude toward Islam in our culture. But I have another worry.

I believe in freedom of religion, and I believe that the deepest and most constructive criticisms come from within one's tradition. So I concentrate on encouraging Christians to be more open to and appreciative of Muslim wisdom in order to be better Christians. But belief in freedom of religion also compels me to express concern about the persecution of Christians.

John L. Allen, associate editor of *Crux: Covering All Things Catholic*, writes regularly about worldwide persecution of Christians. His 2013 book, *The Global War on Christians: Dispatches from the Front Lines of Anti-Christian Persecution*, includes descriptions of appalling treatment of Christians. In 2014, he reported that twenty-six Catholic pastoral workers were killed in the line of duty. This number may sound low. But it is the tip of an iceberg that includes Christians of all denominations as well as imprisoned Christians enduring fates worse than death.

In *Global War*, Allen wrote that an estimated two to three thousand Christians languish in what amount to Eritrean concentration camps. The evangelical group Open Doors publishes an annual World Watch List detailing persecution. Their 2015 report estimates that 100 million Christians face possible persecution. They report that the worst offender for the past thirteen years is North Korea. But then the list shifts to the Middle East and Africa, with Somalia and Iraq as the world's second and third worst persecutors.

Whereas Open Doors emphasizes the role of Islamist extremism in persecution, Allen notes that in the Catholic list of twenty-six deaths in 2014, only two were at the hands of Muslim extremists. The most dangerous country for Catholic pastoral workers in 2014 was Mexico. In another recent article, Allen indicates that "Kidnapping Christian clergy has become a cottage industry among armed factions in Syria."

Christian leaders are crying out for support. After the April 2015 massacre of 147 Christians in Kenya, Bishop Anthony Muheria of Kitui lamented the lack of response from the rest of the world. Visiting Rome after the massacre, Muheria noted how passionately the world responded to the Charlie Hebdo shootings and the May 2015 German plane crash in the French Alps. His question to us is, "Do all lives have equal value?"

By the grace of God, we have ways to help. I have always appreciated the work of the Catholic Near East Welfare Association. You may also be familiar with Aid to the Church in Need.

Historically, Christianity has had a powerful influence on our culture, and many of us may find it difficult to imagine a powerless or persecuted Christian community. But in places as far away as Egypt, Iraq, and Myanmar, and even in traditionally Roman Catholic countries such as Mexico, Christians are suffering. Let us pray for them and find ways to reach out to assure them they are not forgotten.

24
Open Kitchen

The Parliament of the World's Religions

Tessa Bielecki

"Religion may be the problem," said Rabbinit Hadassah Froman from the Holy Land, "but it's also the solution." I agreed, and I suspect, so did the other 9,805 people from eighty countries and three hundred religious traditions who also attended the sixth Parliament of the World's Religions in Salt Lake City October 15-19, 2015.

The first Parliament in 1893, inspired by Swami Vivekananda, drew from three to seven thousand attendees to Chicago and made the West aware of the beauty of Hinduism, Jainism, Buddhism, and Baha'i. A hundred years later, again in Chicago, three thousand people, including the Dalai Lama, explored the ethical common ground shared by the world's spiritual traditions.

Three subsequent Parliaments took place from 1999-2009 in South Africa, Spain, and Australia, with Nelson Mandela, Archbishop Desmond Tutu, Dr. Shirin Ebadi, Dr. Jane Goodall, and President Jimmy Carter attending. The Australian Government issued a national apology to the aboriginal peoples at the fifth Parliament, which convened indigenous elders from around the world.

Indigenous peoples were well represented in Salt Lake, too, in a major plenary session and multiple workshops. On the first day of the Parliament, indigenous peoples lit a Sacred Fire in a sunrise ceremony and kept it burning continuously until the end of the gathering. I loved going to the fire every morning to pray with them before coffee and my first workshop.

Faith in Women and Prayer

One major plenary focused on Faith in Women: Women's Dignity and Human Rights. Only nineteen women addressed the first Parliament in 1893. Over half the presenters at the sixth Parliament in Salt Lake were women, and over sixty percent of the registrants.

I was part of an intergenerational panel of women ranging in age from twenty to seventy-two, representing Christian, Buddhist, Muslim, Sufi, Mennonite, Navajo, and Inter-spiritual traditions. Our theme was Embodied Service: the Wholeness of Women's Spiritual Leadership. I also joined Imam Jamal Rahman and Celeste Yacobani for a session on How Do You Pray: Celebrating the Spirit that Unites Us.

Hope for a World of Compassion

The theme of this Parliament was *Reclaiming the Heart of Our Humanity: Working Together for a World of Compassion, Peace, Justice, and Sustainability.* Plenary speakers and workshop leaders clearly exhibited "faith in action." They were not simply "talking heads" full of abstract theory, but practical and experienced activists "on the ground," offering concrete strategies for Turning Hate Speech into an Opportunity for Bridge Building, Preventing Genocide and Atrocity Crimes, and Raising a Prejudice-Free Child.

One workshop used the experience of St. Francis meeting the Sultan of Egypt as A Model for Peacemaking. Another used lessons from the U.S. Civil Rights Movement as a way of Combatting Islamophobia, Anti-Semitism, and Racial Violence. Dr. Shaik Muhammad Ubaid's session shared Lessons from the Intra-Faith Fight against Violent Extremism. "Every major religion is struggling to contain and defeat violent extremism within," he noted. "The violent extremists share commonalities such as ultra-nationalism and *distortion* of their religious teachings."

A Saturday workshop offered Smart Strategies to Diffuse Terrorism, another addressed Freedom of Speech and Respect for the Other: Looking for Balance, yet another the generational effects of war in Trauma, Death and Dignity: How Faith is a

Source of Strength. I especially appreciated the sessions that dealt with specific areas of the world I know only through the media, such as Dream or Reality: Twenty Years of the Peace Building Process in Bosnia and Herzegovina, The Future of Syria and the Region, Grassroots Women Working across Faith Lines in Conflict Zones (Uganda, Israel, Pakistan, and the Philippines).

Hope in the Holy Land

The Parliament gave considerable attention to grassroots work across faith lines in the Holy Land. Building Sustainable Peace in the Holy Land opened with a description of the principles and practices of the Interfaith Encounter Association, whose efforts build bridges between neighboring communities: sixty-five to date across the Holy Land. Peace-building women from this troubled region offered Faith-Based Techniques and Tools for Trust-Building and had participants prepare action plans to take home.

Hope for Jerusalem outlined a vision for a Center of HOPE, a House of Prayer and Education, a "shared home" in the Holy City where people from all faith traditions can learn from one another and pray side-by-side. NewGround, a Muslim-Jewish Partnership for Change, promoted Relationship Building as an Antidote to Hate. "The media is full of examples of conflict and tension between religious and cultural communities, especially Muslims and Jews," the group points out. "Our world needs more examples of Muslim-Jewish cooperation."

An example of such cooperation is the Healing Quilt hung in the Exhibit Hall at the Parliament. It was created in Jerusalem by seventy-two Palestinian and Israeli women: Jews, Christians, and Muslims. Each piece is in the shape of a hand, a typical Middle Eastern symbol. The seventy-two embroidered, painted, and decorated hands on the quilt are just the beginning, each one representing the voice of one woman envisioning a better and peaceful future for her children.

The Abrahamic Reunion

I was particularly moved by twelve members of The Abrahamic Reunion, the largest interfaith peace organization in the Holy Land, bringing together hundreds of people of different faiths, both men and women, Jews, Muslims, Christians, and Druze, to pray, walk, eat, and study their different scriptures together. The group was founded in 2004 and includes Hadassah Froman and Haji Ibrahim Abu El Hawa, who runs a "peace house" on the Mount of Olives as a gateway of hospitality.

Froman calls the Abrahamic Reunion her family and brings Israeli settlers and Palestinians together in dialogue. "I live in the eye of the storm," she told us. "This is frightening, but the best place to be. Pain comes up, and we deal with it." Her question to her non-Jewish neighbors is, "How can I join you on the path you are taking?"

The Reunion believes the Israeli army should keep peace for both Jewish and Palestinian communities and longs to include soldiers in their work because "the army operates on fear and separation." Hadassah and other Jews help Palestinians get through the bureaucracy of the checkpoints set up by the Israeli Government at the monstrous wall which virtually imprisons the Palestinian people. She told a touching story of making a simple phone call and getting a pregnant Palestinian woman through a checkpoint quickly in the middle of the night; otherwise she would have died in childbirth.

The Bedouin Voice

One of the most powerful voices in the group belonged to Sanaa Albaz, a Bedouin woman from the desert who spoke passionately in Arabic. Frustrated because the secular peace process has not resolved the conflict in her homeland, she found the Abrahamic Reunion and believes the solution will come from religion "for one deep simple reason: we are all created by one God."

I got all choked up when she proclaimed, "When I opened the Qur'an, the Torah, and the New Testament, I found one word: peace." Looking out at the large group crowded into the room (Parliament officials tried to remove those sitting on the floor, but they wouldn't budge), she almost shouted, "I see very sweet faces here. *Look* at me and *listen* to me!"

The use of the word "Reunion" is telling. Members of the group see greater common ground in their *religious* identities than they do in their ethnic or national identities. So they make interfaith peace journeys together, "walking arm in arm and hand in hand, providing an example of love on a small scale." (Doesn't all great change begin in small ways?) The Reunion is convinced that "the political peace process in the Holy Land meets only impasse, whereas [their] faith-based approach builds a lasting foundation for peace" because it opens hearts and creates friendships, trust, and understanding.

Commitments to Peace

These peacemaking efforts in the Holy Land are only a few of many hopeful movements around the world. Why don't we hear more about them? The Parliament helped counter the media's negative mentality ("If it bleeds, it leads") by giving ample time and space to these non-violent movements.

The Forgiveness Project collects stories of forgiveness from around the world into an exhibit called "The F Word" to explore how storytelling, conflict resolution, and dialogue can be used to break cycles of violence and restore hope. Each day of the Parliament I meditated on one of these stories in the Exhibit Hall, inspired by the traumatized men and women who see forgiveness as a heroic act of defiance and a "way to live with the past without being held captive by it."

I love the Golden Rule Project in Salt Lake City and the Formulations of the Golden Rule they collected into four pages from a wide array of cultures, printed in Parliament programs and hung in beautiful banners throughout the Salt Palace.

The initial aim of the Project was to place the Golden Rule in middle and high schools to encourage students to consider it. Then in 2012, the Project commissioned a professional magician to create a performance that combined the Golden Rule message, anti-bullying techniques and educational but dazzling magic effects. *Attention, Magic and the Golden Rule* was born as a positive and transformational experience for older students, with a special adaptation for elementary students.

Your Piece of World Peace

I'm also inspired by the Salt Lake Interfaith Roundtable's efforts to build a Culture of Peace. "You may not be responsible for world peace," they tell us, "but you are responsible for your piece of world peace and your own inner peace." They outline ten foundational principles for a global culture of harmony and encourage us to spend just one week looking at life through the peace-builder lens.

You may also want to investigate International Peace Warriors, Compassion Games (C Games) with its "eleven-day Kindness challenge," and the Compassionate Listening Project, which reaches into the heart of discord and gets underneath triggers and wounds, helping us avoid the Drama Triangle of victim-perpetrator-rescuer and humanize, not demonize the other.

Everyone at the Parliament received a Commitment Book with six declarations related to the six major issues in the plenary sessions. "I will do it. I will lead others to do it!" reads the cover. The booklet provides concrete suggestions for personal and organizational commitments, how to work on policy changes, and how to influence media to become truly fair, socially responsible, independent of corporate interest, and committed to cross-cultural understanding.

As Nelson Mandela said, "Action without vision is only passing time, vision without action is merely day dreaming, but vision with action can change the world."

Islamophobia

Concern over growing Islamophobia and the scapegoating of Muslims in our country led to the creation of the Desert Foundation in 2005. So I was glad to see the Parliament countering worldwide ignorance of Islam with workshops such as The Qur'an: Proclaimer of Tolerance and Lenience, A [Muslim] Declaration against Extremism, Grassroots Interfaith Initiatives to Counter Islamophobia, and Clarifying Misconceptions about Islam, Muslims, and ISIS.

In our post-9/11 world, many Americans conflate the mainstream Muslim majority with the beliefs and actions of an extremist minority. Dr. John Esposito's session was titled Who Speaks for Islam? and answered the question with the empirical evidence of one billion Muslim voices. Explaining Why ISIS is Not Islamic, Hamid Hai said: "ISIS has vitiated the very foundations on which Islamic Law is based. Prophet Muhammad had specifically warned against the rise of such extremist groups which, while having the veneer of Islamic identity, will abrogate the very principles he enunciated."

Why Islam is Not Threatening America

Professor Robert Pape created the first comprehensive database of every suicide terrorist attack in the world from 1980 until today. In *Dying to Win*, Pape provides a groundbreaking demographic profile of modern suicide terrorist attacks. His findings offer a powerful counterpoint to what we now accept as conventional wisdom on the topic. His lecture, Why Islam is Not Threatening America, was based on the most scientific research funded by the Defense Department.

We are reluctant to talk about it, but 9/11 is still hurting America. That day inflicted a wound of public fear that easily reopens with the smallest provocation and continues to bleed the United States of money, lives, and goodwill around the world. Many believe, as I do, that America's response to this fear has inspired more threats and attacks and made us less safe. I congratulate the Parliament for its positive effort towards healing our wound of fear.

Violence or Compassion?

We are often plagued by the notion that religion wounds and divides people instead of bringing them together, partly because we see sacred texts abused and interpreted violently. One workshop I attended put these texts in a more historical and healing context.

Dr. Jonathan Brown, Chair of Islamic Civilization at Georgetown University's School of Foreign Service, represented Islam in a presentation too elaborate for me to summarize well. His major point was this: "No Islamic school read the Qur'an literally until the twentieth century." ISIS and other Muslim extremists take Qur'anic verses out of context to support their false jihadist position.

A Torah of Non-Violence

Rabbi Lynn Gottlieb believes her Jewish people have not recovered from genocide. She insisted that the revered rabbinic tradition has *rejected* the violent passages of the Torah. She teaches "a Torah of non-violence" and began Muslim-Jewish Peace Walks in Albuquerque, which spread across the United States. Young Muslim and Jewish kids who sit around the campfire with her ask, "Why can't the world be like this?"

Dr. Karen Armstrong, a religious historian and former Roman Catholic nun, was the Christian voice. "We read scripture today with a literalness unparalleled in history," she said. We cannot make religion the "scapegoat for the sins of secular society." Our scriptures are violent because "we're violent and we're state builders... All states are founded and maintained by violence." We need to incarnate what our scriptures teach: the Golden Rule, respect for others. "And this can't be confined to your own congenial group."

Responding to questions from the audience, all three panelists became more impassioned and prophetic. "Greed is not kosher," said Rabbi Gottlieb. "We are guilty, America. Give up the male notion of self-defense." "I'm very troubled by the gun culture here," said Dr. Armstrong, urging America to "get this right before you address Muslims about violence."

"ISIS did not exist before 2003," insisted Dr. Brown. "ISIS is the result of our unjust war in Iraq." The audience applauded as he concluded: "Preoccupation with ISIS keeps Americans from reflecting on our government's misactions."

Charter for Compassion International

How do we respond to this? "I'm filled with dread and sorrow," said Dr. Armstrong, "so I do the work of compassion. Compassion is not a nice idea, but an urgent global necessity."

She is the inspiration behind the Charter for Compassion International, a global network to connect individuals, organizations, cities and communities around the world, who make compassion their prime motivation, caring for others and relieving suffering wherever it is found.

A Sabbath of Music and Dance

Of course I didn't attend all the workshops I describe! There were over six hundred programs, so it was mind-boggling to read the catalogue, let alone decide which programs to attend. After three days my head ached, so I took a break on the Sabbath.

I began Sunday morning with Beyond Words: An Interfaith Ritual for Peace, performed by the Omega West Dance Company. I was so happy to sink into my chair, go "non-verbal," and feel the dance ritual unfurl with greetings of peace, exotic chants, and movements from Judaism, Christianity, Islam, Buddhism, Hinduism, and Native traditions, complete with colorful swirling banners and sacred symbols. The dance was choreographed by Carla De Sola, whom I had not seen since her innovative and controversial liturgical dances in the sixties. She described her dance as "social justice" and "a response to hate."

Later in the day I reveled in a concert by the One Voice Children's Choir, enjoying their carefree play in the foyer ahead of time. What can be more uplifting than the bright faces and innocent voices of young children in red singing "It Just Takes Love," showing us that "Friends and song are more important than wealth?"

Sunday evening the Parliament offered a free concert of Sacred Music from around the world at the Mormon Tabernacle, which was far smaller than I expected. I was thrilled to hear a Jewish *shofar*, a Northern Ute flute, and the Muslim Call to Prayer in that space. The Youth Multi-Faith Choir from Salt Lake was a bit chaotic, with all those little Muslim, Hindu, Jewish, Sikh, Buddhist, Christian, Jain, and Baha'i children trying to line up on stage, but they were irresistible in their native dress, singing "We're One Family."

I was stunned by the Cambodian Blessing Dance and the "Whirling Dervishes" from the Mevlevi Order of America. But by far the most moving for me were the drumming refugees from Burundi, who perform to keep their African spirituality alive in their new Utah home. One of the men had survived the massacre in Rwanda. "The drum is the heartbeat of the community," he wrote. Carried in and out on top of the men's heads, the drums were enormous. They made my heart soar, and I could have listened all night.

Open Kitchen

The Sikh religion is the fifth largest in the world. The first Sikh Guru, Nanak Dev Ji, began the tradition of *Langar*, the Sikh word for "open kitchen." At the Golden Temple in India, over 100,000 people are fed for free every single day. The tradition is designed to uphold the Sikh principle of equality between all people, regardless of religion, caste, color, creed, age, gender or social status. Long lines snaked through the Salt Palace for three hours in the middle of every day as local, national, and international Sikh communities cooperated to share this experience of inclusivity with all those who came to the Parliament.

I did not have the patience to wait in line, and I needed the short periods of silence and solitude at noontime to rest my tired brain from the morning's stimulation and prepare for the afternoon. I'm sorry I missed this opportunity. The more I think about it, the more "open kitchen" becomes a metaphor for the Parliament and the planet. Everyone is welcome. Everyone is equal. Food is freely given and received humbly by each one sitting on the earth with bare feet and a reverently covered head.

What does it take to make the whole world an open kitchen? The Parliament of the World's Religions gives us a way to begin.

The Heart's Terrain

Poetry is part of the fabric of the desert, as much a part as sand and rock.

David Jasper

My heart can take on any form…
a cloister for monks…
Ka'aba for the circling pilgrim,
the tables of the Torah,
the scrolls of the Qur'an.
I profess the religion of love.
Wherever its caravan turns
along the way, that is the belief,
the faith I keep.

Ibn al-'Arabi

Prince Hassan bin Talal of Jordan has frequently called to mind the legacy of Muslim Spain and the living heritage of "al-Andalus" as a shining example of how Jewish, Christian, and Islamic civilizations coexisted. From the universal inheritance of Andalusia, he says, we can learn that we have a choice between the way of pluralism (the way of tolerance and understanding) or the way of exclusivism (which leads to tragedy).… Perhaps more than anything else, exclusivism has been the chief cause of bloodshed in human history. In the ruins of Sarajevo we see the negative image of the city of Cordoba.

Karl-Joseph Kuschel

Part 3
Walls and Bridges

Jerusalem, Jerusalem, you who kill the prophets and stone those sent to you, how many times I yearned to gather your children together, as a hen gathers her young under her wings, but you were unwilling!

Matthew 23:37

25
Sabeel

A Spring of Hope

David Denny

Sabeel is an ecumenical, grass-roots, Palestinian Christian movement working for peace in the Middle East. Friends of Sabeel North America has a Colorado chapter. When Tessa Bielecki and I learned of their fact-finding pilgrimage to Israel/ Palestine in May 2007, we decided to go. It was a heartrending yet hopeful excursion. We learned so much from Jewish, Christian, and Muslim peacemakers. You may read more about our trip in the following chapters.

Jesus in Occupied Territory

Our introduction to Sabeel came in the autumn of 2006, when Sabeel invited PLO Mission Ambassador Afif Safiyeh to speak at St. Mary's Cathedral in Colorado Springs. Safiyeh is one of the two percent of Palestinians who are Christian. He spoke about the peace process and recounted the myriad difficulties Palestinians undergo, including the daily loss of eight million man hours, passing through 650 checkpoints, in order to work or go to school or find medical help. I wanted to see firsthand what Safiyeh described. And Sabeel got my attention in a special way by reminding me that Jesus lived in occupied territory.

Sabeel grew out of the Palestinians' longing to understand their situation from a Christian perspective. They were disillusioned with a "spirituality" that taught them that their lot is to suffer. They convened for the first time in 1990 at Bethlehem's Tantur Ecumenical Institute. They now focus their energies on six areas: community, youth, women, clergy, international outreach, and annual events that include ecumenical celebrations.

Sabeel's Ecumenical Liberation Theology Center is located in Jerusalem and provides excellent resources for shedding light on this troubled neighborhood in the Middle East. Friends of Sabeel North America seeks peace and justice in the Holy Land through non-violence and education. They co-sponsor regional educational conferences, alternative pilgrimages, witness trips, and international gatherings in the Holy Land.

The Arabic word *sabeel* means "a way," "a spring" or "a watercourse." It reminds me of the Spanish word *acequia*, an irrigation ditch that brings life-giving water to arid land. Ironically, the word *acequia* derives from the Arabic *al-saqiyah*. The Arab and Berber Muslims of medieval Spain introduced the very irrigation practices that continue today in the American Southwest.

By the grace of God and the brave efforts of both Palestinian and Israeli peacemakers, may living waters flow to a Holy Land thirsting for justice, mercy, and lasting peace.

26
Holy Land Watch

Peace, Not Apartheid

David Denny

When I returned from Israel/Palestine in 2007, I told friends here in the States that the trip was both heartbreaking and hopeful. I notice that my sense of hope wanes as time and distance wax between me and the beautiful, courageous Israelis and Palestinians we met.

When I was there, listening to Angela Godfrey-Goldstein of the Israeli Committee Against House Demolitions (ICAHD), or visiting the Lutheran-sponsored International Center of Bethlehem and watching Palestinian children folk dancing, hearing Dr. Nuha Khoury describe the Center's Dar al-Kalima College or listening to an Israeli Jew and a Palestinian Muslim describe the death of family members and the search for forgiveness, reconciliation and peace, I was buoyed up.

Dr. Khoury's determination to promote creativity and learning, and a Palestinian English teacher's warm welcome to us despite the "security fence" that severs her village, somehow made the approximately four-hundred-mile barrier seem vulnerable.

Before departing for Jerusalem, I read Jimmy Carter's book, *Palestine: Peace, Not Apartheid*, and I was sobered. But in a radio interview Carter said that settlements, the wall, and the occupation are hotly debated within Israeli society. This gave me hope, and our visit to the Holy Land confirmed Carter's contention. We met Eitan Bronstein, for example, whose Zochrot ("Remembering") organization educates Israelis about the history of Palestinian villages that have disappeared from current Israeli maps.

The Colorado Friends of Sabeel sponsored our trip. Sabeel itself is a beacon of hope for the few Christians left in Palestine.

According to their web site, "Sabeel seeks to deepen the faith of Palestinian Christians, to promote unity among them toward social action. Sabeel strives to develop a spirituality based on love, justice, peace, nonviolence, liberation and reconciliation for the different national and faith communities."

Stumbling Towards Political Holiness

This entire experience has confirmed me in my life with the Desert Foundation. Dutch Dominican Edward Schillebeeckx frames this perspective: "Without prayer or mysticism, politics soon becomes cruel and barbaric. Without political love, prayer or mysticism soon becomes sentimental or uncommitted interiority." The monasticism of my earlier years prevented me from involvement with politics. I understood my work as a commitment to silence, solitude, and contemplation, which are generally undervalued in our culture. Contemplative life, in a sense, is already and inherently "political." But this trip tugs me toward a new and painful recognition that Christ breaks down old boundaries in order to lure us into deeper, more difficult, but more accurate responses to his call.

I always admired Thomas Merton's commitment to civil rights and his critique of the Vietnam War. In that context, this shift toward "political love" makes sense, even though those two words seem very strange bedfellows. But if we believe in the Incarnation, then we have to face Schillebeeckx's "political holiness." Not a reunion of Church and State, but the infusion of the art of the possible with a Martin Luther King-like Dream, a Gandhian commitment to "soul force," or the contemporary Jewish commitment to *tikkun,* a Hebrew word that means "to mend, repair, and transform the world." This is not unrealistic or utopian. We have seen what King and Gandhi accomplished.

Yes, my *sense* of hope has waned since returning to our sound-bite culture that either polarizes life and death struggles into black and white or ignores them while focusing on television series finales and celebrity arrests. I was discouraged to learn that in 2006 the United States gave an estimated $2,531,326,000 of military aid to Israel while international aid to Palestine virtually ceased since the Hamas election victory of January 2006. "The idea is to put Palestinians on a diet but not make them die of hunger," commented Dov Weisglass, senior advisor to Israeli Prime Ministers Ariel Sharon and Ehud Olmert. In 2004, "9.9 percent of children under five years of age experienced stunting, 4.9 percent were found to be underweight and 2.8 percent experienced wasting" in Palestine, according to *Bridges: Israeli-Palestinian Public Health Magazine.*

The situation has not improved. In fiscal year 2015 Israel received $3.1 billion in direct bilateral military aid from the United States. This amounts to about $10.2 million per day. A 2015 report from the United Nation's Conference on Trade and Development predicts that Gaza will be uninhabitable by 2020. The United States gives no military aid to Palestine; it did, however, give Palestine $441 million in policing, humanitarian, and development aid in fiscal year 2015.

International law seems to indicate that Israel's occupation of the West Bank is illegal. Occupation must be "temporary, respectful of the humanitarian needs and human rights of the occupied population, and [lead] to an expeditious return to normalcy based on sovereign equality," according to Orna Ben-Naftali, Aeyal M. Gross, and Keren Michaeli, writing for the *Berkeley Journal of International Law* in 2005. But in 2015, New Jersey Governor Chris Christie felt compelled to apologize for referring to the "occupied territories" in a speech he gave before donors to the Republican Jewish Coalition. This term is rejected by many conservative Zionists, who refer to the territory as "disputed."

No Angels, No Demons

In the writings of Polish Solidarity activist Adam Michnik, I read a sage observation: in this world, there are no demons and no angels. In my awkward stumble toward political holiness,

I'm trying to remain within this "real world" of broken human beings who both harm and heal. There are no American, Israeli, or Palestinian angels or demons. This, then, is the source of real hope: the appeal to the *humanity* in each person, that image of God which may be defaced or corroded, but never smothered.

There is a distinction between "desert" and "wasteland." Israel was tested and purified in the Sinai. Jesus resisted temptations to economic, political, and spiritual power in the desert. Muhammad spent his early years in the desert learning the venerable ways of Bedouin life. The desert, then, is a crucible of formation and transformation. But a wasteland is a destructive, noxious environment and ultimately, as T.S. Eliot put it, "unreal." Not that the lamentations of Israeli and Palestinian mothers are unreal. But the lack of vision, the paucity of political love is unrealistic and inadequate.

I fervently pray that the wasteland that eats away at the souls of Israelis, Palestinians, and Americans will become a desert of transformation.

27
Holy Land: Common Ground

A Film by Edward Gaffney and Alicia Dwyer

David Denny

This documentary film introduces faces behind the headlines, Palestinians and Israelis who have lost family members yet choose to resist violent reactions to their grief. Rather, they join together in efforts at healing. We meet a Palestinian family whose car was riddled with bullets one night several years ago near Bethlehem, leaving their teenage daughter dead. (The Israeli soldiers who fired the shots said the car looked like another car the soldiers expected to pass, driven by Palestinian terrorists.)

Israelis Against House Demolitions

We meet Salim and Arabiya Shawamreh, West Bank Palestinians whose home was demolished not only once, but four times. Thanks to the support of folks such as Israeli-American Jeff Halper of the Israeli Committee Against House Demolitions, the fifth house remains as a meeting place for foreign visitors who come to learn about the Israeli occupation, settlement building, and discriminatory housing regulations.

We meet Dalia Landau and Bashir Al-Khayri, who met after the 1967 war, when Bashir went to visit his childhood home in Ramla. Dalia and her family had lived there since 1948, after Bashir's family was expelled and Israel was founded. They became friends, and at one point Dalia considered turning the house over to Bashir. But it is illegal to do so. Instead, together Dalia and Bashir have converted their home into The Open House, a daycare center for Palestinian children and a center where Israeli and Palestinian teenagers meet and talk about their present and future lives together.

We meet several other courageous Israeli and Palestinian parents who have suffered gravely and turned their grief into a persistent pursuit of dialogue, healing, and peace. One Palestinian man describes how his dead son's organs were donated to seven Israeli children. In this way, the father says, he has lost one child, gained seven, and through these children, he has, in a sense, returned to his native land.

A South African Israeli mother describes her grief over the loss of her son, an Israeli soldier. Her encounter with the mother of the little girl killed in the mistakenly identified car is unforgettable. The pain is so great that these parents are able to ignore the camera completely. We are swept into a deep and heartbreaking intimacy with their plight and experience a sober hope.

28
Jerusalem Sky

Stars, Crosses, and Crescents

Tessa Bielecki

Simple children's books are sometimes deep inspiration for adults. This is true of *Jerusalem Sky*, written and illustrated by Dr. Mark Podwal.

This beautiful book begins, "With wonders and miracles, the sky over Jerusalem touches the world below.... Legend says that the Jerusalem sky has a hole in it, made by a jewel that fell from God's throne. Through this hole, hopes reach heaven." If the world ever needed hopes to reach heaven from Jerusalem, it is now.

Whose City Is It?

Podwal's publisher initially found the book "too Jewish, too inaccessible." Does this convey the major problem with the ancient sacred city of Jerusalem? Whose city is it anyway? The Jews'? The Christians'? The Muslims'?

After visiting Jerusalem in 2003, Podwal said that he finally understood the city's common significance. This is clearly indicated in both his profound text and magnificent watercolors of "synagogue stars, church crosses, mosque moons." The book's subtitle, *Stars, Crosses, and Crescents,* sums up the centrality of this holy city for all three Abrahamic traditions, for all three "Peoples of the Book."

"Jerusalem is so loved it has seventy names," Podwal writes. "Though it is called City of Peace, no place has been fought over more. Seventeen times torn apart and rebuilt." With searing wisdom and insight, he concludes: "Perhaps possessing Jerusalem is like trying to own the sky."

I loved the descriptions of Jerusalem through its morning and midnight moods and the four seasons of the year: "Every autumn gust tossing a leaf, every winter cloud storming overhead, every spring breeze rustling a treetop, every summer rainbow promising sunshine, is said to be born in the Jerusalem sky."

Middle Eastern Colors

This little volume is only twenty-eight pages long. With very few words and the vibrant colors of the Middle East—blue, orange, purple and gold—Podwal illustrates the importance of the holy city for Jews, Christians, and Muslims:

"Jewish sages tell how, night after night, a full moon shone while Solomon was king. Under his rule the Temple was built... enemies burned down the Temple... By the stones that remain, Jews still pray."*

"Christians tell of a wondrous star in the Jerusalem sky, which brightened the winter night, announcing the news of Jesus' birth. And they tell how thirty-three years later, a spring afternoon's daylight blackened into starless night when Jesus died on a small jagged hill, now crowned by a great church."

"Muslims tell of the prophet Muhammad's night journey in which midnight glowed like day when he rode through the sky on a flying horse, then reached heaven on a stairway of light. Where Muhammad rose to heaven now stands a mosque with sky blue stones and a dome of gold shining like a second sun."

Podwal's two-page drawing of this Dome of the Rock is the most striking in the book. It also conveys his remarkable openness, since the structure, built in the seventh century C.E. on the former Jewish Temple mount, is a source of tension for many other Jews.

Podwal is a dermatologist. When not drawing, he serves as a clinical associate professor at New York University School of Medicine. An accomplished artist, his work has appeared in the *New York Times* for over thirty years and is also represented in the Metropolitan Museum of Art.

Jerusalem Sky was a two-year effort for Dr. Podwal and a soul-searching experience for him. "Sometimes I can spend a night finding the right word," he confessed.

A unique project was sponsored by the Anti-Defamation League when the book was first published. Fourth and fifth graders from Jewish, Roman Catholic, and Muslim schools in Brooklyn were each given a copy of the book and asked to create their own artworks showing Jerusalem's importance to all three of the world's major monotheistic religions.

As Marty Markowitz, president of the Brooklyn borough, read the book aloud to the children in a final ceremony, he donned in succession a yarmulke, a cleric's collar (unfortunate, since this is not a symbol of prayer), and a Muslim prayer cap.

Opening the Door

One young Jewish girl did a portrait of a golden-domed synagogue. Her explanation is a source of hope for all of us: "It reminded me of a dream I once had, where there was a door, and behind the door the whole world was at peace. I hope that everyone together can open that door some day."

"Too many people have a one-dimensional view of Jerusalem," said Dr. Podwal with tears in his eyes. These students "made it three-dimensional."

The remaining western wall in Jerusalem is not from the original temple built by Solomon but the temple rebuilt by King Herod in 20 B.C.E.

29

A Bedouin Feminist

Out of the Negev Desert

David Denny

Amal Elsana Alh'jooj is an Israeli native and a Bedouin from the desert. She was her parents' fifth daughter. They had no sons. Traditional Bedouin families prize sons more than daughters, and Amal's mother wondered whether her father would find a second wife who might give him sons. She couldn't stop crying. Her husband assured the mother of his daughters that he would not take a second wife. He named this fifth child Amal, which means "Hope," trusting in whatever Allah provides.

"You're a Girl"

Over the next years, Amal's mother gave birth to five sons! But Amal says she was raised as a boy as much as a girl. She was a shepherd at five years old. When her brothers began heading to Haifa for college, she expected to go, too. But her father said, "No, not you. You're a girl." Her place was in the home. She knew that "something unfair was happening" around her and began, as she put it, to "revise my image of the tribe." She set out to change her tribe.

First Bedouin Women's Group

At age seventeen, aware that Bedouin men received credit for work often accomplished by women, Amal founded the first Bedouin women's group. She also convinced her father to send her to college. Because of this, her father's car was burned. The following year an Israeli journalist asked if she was a "feminist." She had never heard the word. The journalist said that feminists work for equal rights for women. Amal said, "Thank you very much. This is me!" But when her photograph appeared in newspapers as the first Bedouin woman to attend university, it brought "shame" on her family.

Amal speaks fondly of her father, who broke with tradition in order to support his radical daughter. He, too, had never heard the word "feminist." A friend told him that feminists were American women who danced in the streets and burned their bras in public. But by acting to improve her community, Amal dispelled this ignorant caricature. She learned an invaluable lesson: if she truly loves her community, respects and listens to its members, they will not excommunicate her.

Amal was honored at the second annual Seeking Common Ground: Circles of Change awards breakfast in Denver. She manifested an attitude I witnessed on our fact-finding visit to Israel/Palestine sponsored by Friends of Sabeel Colorado: Amal refuses to see herself or her community as victims. She said it would be easy to cry over her people's minority status, over the injustices meted out to her unrecognized village in the Negev. Instead, since 2000, she has worked with the Negev Institute for Strategies of Peace and Development and NISPED's Arab-Jewish Center for Equality, Empowerment and Cooperation (AJEEC) to achieve equal human and civil rights in Israel.

Amal trusts that deep inside, Jewish and Palestinian Israelis seek justice and cooperation. The gap between these two communities is so great that although they share the same land, members of one community can live without ever meeting the other. Noting that for most Israeli Arabs and Jews, there are only two spaces: "ours" and "theirs," Amal set out to create a "third space" shared between Jews and Arabs in an atmosphere of respect, understanding, and equal opportunity.

Conversations between Neighbors

She believes that development is not about physical structures; it is about people and attitudes. Nor is she interested in a revolution against anyone. Instead, she encourages a process, a conversation between neighbors. Giving citizens a chance to say what they need and creating ways to meet those needs opens new spaces of cooperation and hope. Work accomplished at the grass roots level heightens people's sense of ownership, which leads to good stewardship. Amal's attitude and work must be contagious: in her years with NISPED and AJEEC, the number of volunteers has grown from forty-seven to three hundred fifty. And now almost five hundred Bedouin women attend university.

30
View from the Rooftop

"If I forget you, O Jerusalem…"

Tessa Bielecki

This is my last morning in Jerusalem. For the first time in my two-week sojourn, I slept through the cries of the muezzins, beginning at 3:40 A.M., amplified by multiple microphones. I awake instead to the cooing of the doves outside my window, under the pomegranate tree in the garden of the Lutheran Guesthouse.

I dress quickly, not wanting to miss a minute, and go up to the rooftop to greet the day and salute the holy city. Jerusalem is usually noisy, but dawn has not yet come, and most of the city still sleeps. It is quiet except for the gentle sounds of nature. Swallows twitter and fly between the rooftops. The doves continue cooing to one another. The ravens call softly, not as raucously as they do in Colorado.

Wind blows through the trees in the garden and rustles the leaves of the purple-blossomed jacaranda, the palms, the locust and the loquat, the tiny olive and the majestic fig. I marvel at the bright colors of the hollyhocks, nasturtiums, and oleanders. I smell lavender and the red geraniums.

Food and Flowers

A rooster crows as I thank God for another day, for this remarkable journey, and for the rooftops, one of the wonders of life in the Middle East, along with hummus, tomatoes and cucumbers for breakfast! Next door a young Palestinian is already talking on his cell phone. Across the way a Greek Orthodox priest hangs his freshly washed black robe out to dry. Below me a pious Jew, wrapped in his prayer shawl, takes a shortcut over the roofs to his morning prayers at the "Wailing" or Western Wall.

The homier rooftops feature lush flower pots and oriental rugs. Lavish deep pink bougainvillea spills over the wall to the south. Someone on the west side has even planted a grape arbor. Caper bushes stubbornly push out of numerous nooks and crannies in the stone. I discover, to my utter delight, that the capers we eat, usually in seafood dishes, though the plant comes from the desert, is not a berry after all but an unopened bud. The caper flower is delicate and exquisite. I photographed one in the rocks at Masada and another at Tabga, where we believe Jesus cooked fish on the beach for his disciples after he rose from the dead. Tabga is one of the quieter holy sites, and therefore one of my favorites.

Jewish "Settlements" in the Arab Quarter

The old city of Jerusalem is "one square mile of religion." Someone once said it "stinks of religion," and on some days I feel rather than smell the truth of that. I look out at lovely minarets, crowned with their evocative stars and crescents, at the black domes of the Church of the Holy Sepulcher, and the tall bell tower of the Lutheran Church of the Redeemer. I climbed the tower yesterday, all the way up the winding staircase, suffering stifling claustrophobia in the narrow passageway. But what a spectacular view in all four directions at the top, above the massive bells, which rang while I was there and almost deafened me.

At this hour the utilitarian solar panels, water tanks, satellite dishes, and TV antennas steal nothing of the magic of the ancient white stones of the old city, streets as well as roofs and walls. I am sobered by the number of Israeli flags and the barbed wire around Jewish "settlements," incursions into the Christian and Arab quarters of the city. Outside the walls of the old city lie the unappealing concrete, glass, and steel high rises of modern West Jerusalem. Marring the skyline of this "secular" state, unsightly cranes indicate extensive new construction.

At 6 A.M. the Christian church bells begin to ring out the Angelus, more synchronized than the cacophonous calls of the muezzins. Soon afterwards, the sun rises beyond the pines and eucalyptus on the Mount of Olives. It is a bright and blinding orb in today's hazy sky, illuminating the Hebrew University on Mount Scopus, the tower of Augusta Victoria Hospital, the onion domes of St. Mary Magdalene's, the stark and treeless Jewish cemetery on the Mount of Olives, and closer to me, the golden Dome of the Rock.

I can just barely see my favorite church in the Holy Land, Dominus Flavit, the site where Jesus wept over Jerusalem as we read in the Gospel of Matthew: "Jerusalem, Jerusalem, you that kill the prophets and stone those who are sent to you!" Jesus must weep even more today over Jerusalem and all of Israel/ Palestine, as I weep this morning as well.

Eroding Israel's Moral Fabric

On my last day here, this is the first day I don't have to go early to the bus for heavily scheduled visits with Palestinians suffering under the occupation of the West Bank and brave Israeli human rights groups struggling to relieve that suffering and build a better Israeli society. One such group, New Profile: Movement for the Civilization of Israeli Society, opposes the

Occupation on three counts: 1) its destruction of Palestinian life, society, land, and property, 2) its role in maintaining militarism in Israel, 3) its erosion of Israeli socio-economic and moral fabric. New Profile, along with other Israeli peace groups, seeks "non-violent means of ending this catastrophic Occupation" by "using economic sanctions to pressure the government to change its policy."

In one official statement, the group contends that "ending the occupation is not only to the benefit of the Palestinians but also necessary for the welfare of Israel, its youth, and future generations. Over twenty thousand Israeli soldiers have died in wars since 1948. Enough. It is time to beat our swords into ploughshares, to bring security to Israel by giving the Palestinians their freedom and recognizing their absolute right to exist, and to build a future for today's Israeli youth and generations to come by creating a civilian society whose underpinnings are equality of gender and ethnicity and universal human rights."

This is by far the best of my three trips to the Holy Land. On the first two visits in 1989 and 2000, the undercurrents of unrest and injustice went unaddressed, yet palpably infected the pilgrimages. This time we addressed the painful conflicts head-on, and that made all the difference. Until this "fact-finding" trip, I had no idea so many Israelis are opposed to the Occupation and work on behalf of Palestinian human rights, for the sake of Israel as well.

"Refuseniks" and Women in Black

We met with Rabbis for Human Rights, with "Refuseniks," veteran Israeli soldiers who refuse to serve in the West Bank and help younger soldiers recognize their right to make the same protest for the sake of true national security, and with Machsom Watch, a group of Israeli women who monitor some of the hundreds of military checkpoints to assist Palestinians who may be harassed not only by soldiers but by Israeli "settlers." Many babies have been born at the checkpoints, and several people have died because they were not allowed to pass through for urgent medical care.

We also visited a refugee camp, hospitals and schools, B'Tselem, the Israeli Center for Human Rights in the Occupied Territories, and the Christian Peacemakers Team in Hebron, which escorts Palestinian children to school to protect them from hostilities.

On Friday we stood as witnesses with the Israeli Women in Black, who hold signs with only one simple message in Hebrew, Arabic, and English: End the Occupation. The women mourn for victims on both sides of the conflict and suffer tremendous verbal abuse from passing cars and pedestrians on the busy street corner.

Bereaved Families Network

The most moving encounter was with the Bereaved Families Network, a group of Israelis and Palestinians who have lost loved ones in the recurring violence. Grief helps them move beyond their differences and bond as brothers and sisters, true children of a common father, Abraham, in a common land they share. Israeli-Palestinian pairs travel throughout Israel and the world to be living witnesses to the reality of peace.

Part of the problem is that many Israelis and Palestinians live in complete isolation from one another and never meet. As one Palestinian girl said: "I never thought in my whole life that I would meet 'the other side' or talk to them.... I cannot describe how thankful I am." Her Israeli counterpart agreed: "Can you imagine what it is like for me, a Jewish Israeli teenage girl, that had never met a Palestinian before, and who only lives a few miles away from them.... A magical wave of hope filled my whole body and I hope this feeling never leaves me."

We also took time to visit various holy sites: Church of the Nativity in Bethlehem, Mount of the Beatitudes and the Sea of Galilee, the Tomb of the Patriarchs and Matriarchs, Church of the Annunciation in Nazareth, the Via Dolorosa and Holy Sepulcher in Jerusalem, Jericho, Qumran, Masada, the Dead Sea and Mount of the Temptations in the glorious Judean Desert.

A Colonial Land Grab

Everywhere we went we ran into the illegal "Wall" that is suffocating Palestinian life and "shaming" Israel, as some say. In what some Israelis call a "colonial land grab," the Wall takes land from the Palestinian side, requires the bulldozing of thousands of ancient olive trees, essential for the Palestinians' livelihood, deprives people of their own water, which they then must buy back from Israel, and keeps them locked inside, cut off from health care, schools, markets, and even their own families and fields. Some villages are completely surrounded by the wall where a single nineteen-year-old armed soldier has the power to close the gate and lock in forty thousand people. One Palestinian leader told us it's easier for him to go to Europe than past the wall into Israel.

International Law

In July of 2004, the International Court of Justice ruled that the building of the Wall violates International Law and called on the international community to refrain from any assistance that promotes this violation in any way. According to the ruling, "construction of the wall within the Occupied Territories severely impedes the Palestinian people's right to self-determination and is therefore a breach of Israel's obligation to respect that right." The Court announced that all states are therefore obliged:

1. not to recognize the illegal situation resulting from the Wall and not to render aid or assistance in maintaining the situation created by such construction (passed by a vote of thirteen to two),

2. to insure compliance by Israel with international humanitarian law as embodied in the [Geneva] Convention (passed by a vote of thirteen to two),

3. to bring to an end the illegal situation resulting from the construction of the Wall and the associated regime, taking due account of the present Advisory Opinion (passed by a vote of fourteen to one).

"Stop the Racist Wall"

Grafitti on both sides of the Wall tells the true story: "Shame on you Israel." "Thou shalt not steal." "From the Warsaw Ghetto to the Abu-Dis [name of a Palestinian village] Ghetto." "Stop the racist wall." "Paid for by the USA." Entry into Bethlehem through the Wall ironically proclaims "Peace be with you" from the Israeli side, a "peace" maintained with guard towers, razor wire, and soldiers with machine guns.

I was inspired by the heroism of all the Israeli peacemakers who work so hard to wake up their fellow citizens and influence the government to correct its injustices and create a truly viable society. Many feel that the present situation is unsustainable, largely because it erodes the very soul of Israel.

I was also inspired by the heroism of the Palestinian peacemakers who work so hard to maintain their dignity in the face of such grave injustice. The motto of one school reads: "Destruction may be…. Creativity will be." T-shirts at one of the refugee camps proclaim the indomitable spirit of the people: "to dream together, to work together, to decide together, to build a future together."

Nurturing Hope

As the administrator of one health care center beseeched us, "Please see us as normal human beings, not as traumatized Palestinians under occupation. We are learning coping techniques to 'normalize' our lives and consider them 'good.'" In the spirit of John 10:10, the people of Bethlehem especially believe that they "deserve life and life abundantly." "We nurture hope," said one teacher. "If we lose our hope, we lose our humanity."

I feel profoundly changed by this journey and want to help the Holy Land by helping to remove "walls" and build bridges. As a Palestinian Christian woman at the Sabeel Ecumenical Liberation Theology Center said, "We cannot be true to serving God without politics." According to American Rabbi Michael Lerner, "Politics is a manifestation of the spiritual and ethical consciousness of humanity." Having focused on spirituality for more than half my life, I want to manifest the more political dimension of that spirituality, which Fr. Dave describes as "political love." As we pray in Psalm 137, "If I forget you, O Jerusalem, may my right hand wither."

31
Grief Work

A Palestinian and Israeli in Conversation

David Denny

Two men from two different worlds, separated by a street, a checkpoint, a wall and, until recently, a worldview. One was a tall, slim young Israeli Ashkenazi Jew named Guy. On this night he entered the Old City of Jerusalem through Jaffa Gate the way an American walks into a familiar neighborhood in Boston or Chicago.

The other man was a middle-aged physician named Omar. He felt less confident entering the Holy City. Until 1995, he knew Israelis only as enemy soldiers or as settlers who took lives and land that he loved. At each checkpoint on the way to Jerusalem, he had to present a pass, like a student's permission slip, indicating when he could enter and when he had to depart.

Common Bereavement

Guy and Omar traveled to the Lutheran Guest House in Jerusalem as representatives of the Parents Circle–Families Forum, a grassroots organization of bereaved Palestinians and Israelis. Omar spoke first. He recounted having been displaced from Hebron to Bethlehem to Ramallah, where he now lives and works. In 1972 his father was killed by the Israel Defense Force. Omar's school principal did not inform him of his father's death. He simply sent Omar home to his mother, six sisters and eleven brothers. Two days later, Israeli troops demolished his house. The family spent the next three years in a refugee camp.

In following years, one of Omar's brothers was killed by Israeli forces. But five of his sisters went to university and six siblings became doctors. Two other siblings became pharmacists, one an engineer and one a businessman. Omar went to medical school in Romania, but the Israeli government prevented him from returning home. He spent twenty years in exile in Jordan, where he volunteered in a refugee camp. After returning to Israel, he was imprisoned in the Sinai and then released. During one Ramadan, soldiers burst into his home while his family was feasting and placed Omar under house arrest, which lasted for two years.

Disillusioned with political leadership, Omar concluded that hope lay in conversing with the enemy. Through conversations rooted in common bereavement, he discovered his Israeli neighbors' humanity. On this night, he did not talk about his emotional response to the deaths of his father and brother and his own years of exile. He struck me as weary, reserved, melancholy. But his words and gestures also radiated a physician's compassion and wisdom forged from profound darkness.

Dialogue Begets Dialogue

When Guy spoke, he revealed that ten years earlier, when he was eighteen and newly recruited into the Israeli army, a suicide bomber killed his sister. Guy became convinced that his sister's death was the result of Israeli policies toward Palestinians. He decided that fighting in Lebanon might help him become "normal" again. Maybe killing Arabs would be consoling. But Guy's mother had the right to prevent her only surviving child from going into combat, so Guy was denied this path.

After he left the military, Guy spent five years outside Israel. He lived in the United States and France. In France he met Palestinians and North Africans and realized that he was a Middle Easterner, not a European. After earning a diploma in France, he returned to Israel and learned Arabic on the streets of East Jerusalem. Then he discovered the Parents Circle.

Guy said he believes that just as violence begets violence, "dialogue begets dialogue." He complained of the way the Israeli Defense Department "adopts" those who have lost loved ones to terrorists, offering them financial support and later informing them when government forces have avenged the family's loss. Guy's family rejected such offers, refusing to believe that vengeance heals.

The "Other's" Human Face

After telling their stories, Omar and Guy began to articulate their common concerns. Omar lamented the media's focus on violence. He urged Americans to press the United States government to promote peace and stop the sale of arms. He reported that through more than a thousand lectures to over 25,000 students in Israel and Palestine, the Parents Circle has shown families how they may use their experience of suffering to stop the cycle of revenge. Hope, Guy said, lies "in human contact with the human face of the 'other.'" Then he added, "We don't die of listening."

I have often thought about Omar and Guy heading home through the narrow streets of Jerusalem that night. Omar's and Guy's dead remain dead. Other soldiers have replaced Guy. Omar still presents his pass to a soldier.

The late Palestinian scholar Edward Said said that peace would be possible only when Palestinians and Israelis could sit together, listen to each other's grief, and trust that the other is telling the truth. We don't die of listening. I pray that these two men do not die before their listening bears fruit.

32

Pope Francis at the Wall

"Bethlehem look like Warsaw Ghetto"

Tessa Bielecki and David Denny

On his first trip to the Holy Land in 2014, Pope Francis stunned the world in an "unscripted moment" by asking his driver to stop at the contentious concrete barrier separating Bethlehem from Jerusalem, where he touched his head against the graffiti-covered wall and prayed.

Perhaps he'd been drawn by the spray-painted pleas, "Pope, we need some 1 to speak about justice" and "Bethlehem look like Warsaw Ghetto." Abe Greenhouse from Jewish Voice for Peace reported that the words had been written only moments before. "One day earlier, young Palestinians had also covered the gray behemoth with messages to the Pope, only to find the wall painted over just hours later. Until the moment the Pope arrived, it seemed that Palestinian voices were once again to be silenced."

Francis had already made history by traveling to the Holy Land with a Jewish rabbi and a Muslim imam, longtime friends and collaborators from his days as archbishop of Buenos Aires. Then he became the first pontiff to fly directly into the West

Bank and refer to the Israeli-occupied territory as the "State of Palestine," spotlighting the Vatican's support for the 2012 United Nations resolution that upgraded the Palestinians' status to observer state.

"Monstrous" Walled Ghetto

Palestinians and friends of Palestine loathe the wall, which President Mahmoud Abbas has called "monstrous." Israel insists the wall is essential to its security. But according to Sydney Levy, also from Jewish Voice for Peace, eighty-five percent of the wall's planned four-hundred-mile route is on confiscated Palestinian land. "It enables the annexation of land for illegal settlements and separates Palestinians from their land, teachers and students from schools, and families from each other."

"As Jews," Greenhouse says, "we find walled ghettos uniquely disturbing. As human beings, we find the Pope's decision to draw the eyes of the world to this reality profoundly moving.... In the moment Pope Francis stood for all the cameras to see, the wall became more than a prison wall. It became a message to the outside world showing clearly the reality that Israel tries to hide."

Jewish Voice for Peace, one of our Abrahamic partners, asked us to join over ten thousand others around the world and sign a petition thanking Pope Francis to help inspire other leaders "not to look away."

Both the Israeli and Palestinian presidents responded to the Pope's invitation to join him at his simple Vatican apartment in prayer for peace. According to Oded Ben Hur, a former Israeli ambassador to the Holy See, by personally inviting the presidents to a prayer summit, "Francis eschewed Vatican protocol and tradition while showing atypical boldness. Most pontiffs don't rock the boat." This Pope does.

A Voice, the Spirit,
a Caravan

A voice cries out:
in the desert prepare the way of the Lord!
Make straight in the desert a highway for our God!

Isaiah 40:3

At once the Spirit drove him out into the desert, and he
remained in the desert for forty days, tempted by Satan. He
was among wild beasts, and the angels ministered to him.

Mark 1:13

Come, come, whoever you are.
Wanderer, worshiper,
Lover of leaving—it doesn't matter.
Ours is not a caravan of despair.
Come, even if you have broken your vows
A hundred times, a thousand times.
Come, come again, come.

Jalal al-Din Rumi

Part 4

The Inner Desert

The inner desert arises primarily from grief: the
universal desert of unchosen loss and death, pain that
grinds the soul to dust and bears within it the threat
of despair as well as hope for transformation and
compassion.

David Denny

Dangerous Territory

Disease, Death, and the Desert

David Denny

*O*ff and on in the years since Belden Lane wrote *The Solace of Fierce Landscapes,* I have sampled it and gleaned gems here and there. But this time around, I gained a profound sense of its power as a whole. How to account for that? As the Greeks put it, the only way to *mathos*, understanding, is through *pathos,* suffering. Another way to say it may be that after thirty years in a *voluntary* desert, I was faced with some *involuntary* deserts. A big difference.

Lane tackles three themes in this book: facing grief over his mother's final illness, his instinctive need for solitude and wilderness during his time of grief, and the role of wilderness in the history of Christian spirituality. The beauty in such an approach is that if you are drawn to any single theme, you will discover its intimate connection with the other two.

From Weeping to Waiting

After the drama of his mother's bout with cancer, Lane describes the shift to a long season of waiting, in which his mother slips into Alzheimer's disease. Instinctively, he heads to the wilderness, where he finds that the earth simultaneously ignores and absorbs his grief. And the desert shares his thirst.

As he returns repeatedly to his mother's room at the nursing home, he begins to perceive it as her monastic cell. Together, he and his mother move through the traditional stages of spiritual growth: the *purgation* of wrestling with death, loss, grief and the grotesque human condition; the *illumination* that dawns only gradually as they move through the "ordinary time" of waiting, adjusting to life's limits, moving through anguish and anger and unexpected gifts; the *union* or profound reconciliation between the "true story" of one's broken life and the truer love story through which fear, grief, loss and prayer lead to freedom, laughter, healing of memory, and service.

A Muddy Baptism

Lane gives memorable accounts of his excursions to Mount Sinai and Mount Tabor in the Holy Land, New Mexico's Ghost Ranch, Arkansas' Upper Moss Creek, and Christ in the Desert Benedictine monastery, also in New Mexico.

For me, the most dramatic is his account of hiking up a box canyon at Ghost Ranch. After a mild morning's hike, Lane rests on a rock in a stream. Clouds gather. He scrambles to a small cave in the canyon wall. "Soon sheets of water begin to pour over the top of the canyon rim, loosening the dirt and rocks high above. Then the sound of falling boulders echoed through the canyon like shotgun blasts, crashing right before me onto the path I'd followed an hour or so before." After the cloudburst he undergoes a "baptism" before his return to the ranch:

Dark red waters flowed down from the side canyon to join the light-tan waters from the upper creek, flowing side by side, then merging together in some great mystery. The new waters entering the creek were a deep, chocolate red, the runoff of multicolored mesas from above. They formed a menstrual flow, these dark waters, as if the land were cleansing itself of its life-giving blood. Viscous and thick, they poured especially heavy from between two large boulders. I climbed over to the place, cupped my hands, and let the waters fall over my head, rolling down my hair and onto my shoulders.

Lane's personal accounts and lush descriptions, combined with his anguished need to deal with the deaths of his parents, provide an urgent desperation that drives his well-researched exploration of the Christian tradition of *apophatic* prayer, or wordless, imageless stillness. "This search for the broken Christ in the fields of emptiness," he confesses, "is what has driven me in this work." Late in the book, I believe him when he claims, "What little expertise I can offer to legitimate these words lies less in the training of a scholar than in the perseverance of the *compañero,* one who has traveled with another through dangerous territory."

On Learning I Have Terminal Cancer
Oliver Sacks

I am face to face with dying.... It is up to me now to choose how to live out the months that remain to me. I have to live in the richest, deepest, most productive way I can.... I feel intensely alive, and I want and hope in the time that remains to deepen my friendships, to say farewell to those I love, to write more, to travel if I have the strength, to achieve new levels of understanding and insight.... I feel a sudden clear focus and perspective. There is no time for anything inessential. I must focus on myself, my work and my friends. I shall no longer look at "NewsHour" every night. I shall no longer pay any attention to politics or arguments about global warming....

I cannot pretend I am without fear. But my predominant feeling is one of gratitude. I have loved and been loved; I have been given much and I have given something in return; I have read and traveled and thought and written. I have had an intercourse with the world, and the special intercourse of writers and readers. Above all, I have been a sentient being, a thinking animal, on this beautiful planet, and that in itself has been an enormous privilege and adventure.

The New York Times, February 19, 2015

34
Holy Dying

Jessica MacMaster Danson: 1916-2006

Tessa Bielecki

*My beautiful friend Jessica Danson died January 11, 2006.
I sat by her bedside for the last ten days of her life and kept
this journal. I hope the example of her holy death inspires you,
whether you are on the threshold of death yourself, or close to
someone who is.*

Day 1: January 2

It feels as if a hole is tearing open in the depths of my
soul, and the bottom is falling out of my life. I feel groundless
and bereft. Then I remember: Jessica is dying. That's why the
cruise control is set on eighty, and I am passing all the semi-
trucks on I-40 through the deserts of New Mexico and northern
Arizona. I must get to Sedona in time to see Jess alive and tell
her "good-bye" and "I love you, dearest of friends."

Last year at this time we celebrated a lavish Middle Eastern
Epiphany feast on the Persian rugs in Jessica's bedroom. This
year Jessica is on her way to another celebration. "So, our
Epiphany feast wasn't good enough last year?" I teased her,
"And this year you need to feast at the heavenly banquet?" She
replied, "It would be hard to top last year — only in heaven."

Fr. Dave celebrated Mass at her bedside as soon as we
arrived after the ten-hour drive. I asked Jessica if she wanted
the Epiphany liturgy, but she chose the Transfiguration. (Her
grandmother had died on Transfiguration.) I sang "My soul is
longing for your peace" at Communion. After Mass Jessica
asked for another song, and her daughter Jan suggested St.
Teresa's prayer, "Let nothing disturb you."

Afterwards, an exquisite farewell ritual unfolded
spontaneously. Jan made the first move and kissed her mother
good-bye, then Ted, Jess's sister Eileen, age ninety-one,

granddaughters Kate and Katrina, then the rest of us. Jan spoke about how "one-ed" we were, as Jessica so deeply desired. Ted shared vulnerably about how he felt experiencing such intense reality at his mother's deathbed and then such flatness away from it.

Jessica asked me to explain the meaning of the Transfiguration. I began with Gerard Manley Hopkins's poetry: "The world is charged with the grandeur of God." We don't always see the grandeur, but in the Transfiguration on Mount Tabor, Jesus reveals the mystery to us, as he shimmers in all his glory. Peter can't handle so much dazzling light, so he wants to build a tent and control and contain the mystery.

I thanked Jessica for being such a great example, transfiguring the world around her with such joy and love, peace and beauty, even now, as she lies dying, gathering us together, enfolding us all in her love, and uniting us with one another on ever deepening levels. She is dying as she lived.

Joyce said she was glad Jessica was going to the happiness of heaven, but that we would all weep after she was gone. I said that I would miss her in the flesh so much, despite how I treasure life in the spirit. Jessica responded by telling everyone that she used to live too much in the realm of spirit until her encounter with me and the Spiritual Life Institute, which helped ground her in the sacredness of the earth and the body.

I also told her I envied her going to heaven and meeting my mother, St. Teresa, and Tate, our Sedona cat, who died at age twenty-two. Her grandson Eric piped up, "And Grampy singing 'Oh what a beautiful morning!'"

There were more expressions of love, gratitude and awe, and more tears, in an atmosphere of incredible intimacy. Then we let Jessica rest as we enjoyed one of Joanna's fine dinners together around the table, with more sharing.

Jan showed me the notebook she was compiling of Jessica's last words: profound, funny, other-centered, showing how grounded in the real Jessica is, peaceful and happy about dying, and very ready: "I won't sleep well at night until God comes for me." "I've prepared all my life for dying." "When you think of the hugeness I'm facing, I can't believe it. I am excited!"

She dictated a letter to William McNamara on New Year's Day: "Dear Fr. William, I have neglected you. I will take you into heaven with me. Doctors say I am dying and I hope I will be in peace soon. All my love, Jessica."

Fr. Dave and I left quietly after kissing Jess good night, thinking we might not see her again.

Day 3: January 4

Before Fr. Dave left for Tucson to see his family today, we visited Jessica briefly and prayed the prayer of St. Elizabeth of the Trinity, which Jessica has always loved. It has been so meaningful for me, too, over the years, but the last lines are even more powerful as Jessica is dying: "O my Three, my all, my beatitude, infinite solitude, immensity in which I lose myself, I yield myself up to You as a prey; bury Yourself in me, that I may bury myself in You, while awaiting the time to go and contemplate in Your light the abyss of Your greatness. Amen."

Day 4: January 5

Today I went for a hike into the red rocks, sat on a large slab of Coconino sandstone and sobbed with grief over losing Jessica as my mother, sister, and friend. I don't want to grieve around the deathbed, so Jessica knows she can let go. I had intended to be gone for only an hour, but on the way back I got hopelessly lost (I was disoriented anyway), and could not find my way in the tangle of scrub oak, manzanita, and cat claw acacia. I finally came to a house and met a young man who generously hiked out with me and put me on the path again. Jessica wanted us to come and sing Compline tonight instead of waiting for tomorrow night. "Perfect," she said, after the final blessing. "It makes me weep with joy. So many memories of Compline with you over the years."

Day 5: January 6

I'm glad we prayed Compline together last night and didn't wait. At 9:30 this morning, Jan called to say Jessica was considerably weaker, and we should come right away. Everyone gathered in the bedroom, and it seemed certain that Jessica wouldn't live out the day. Feast of Epiphany: a good day to make the final journey. Jessica agreed and is so ready to go, but she keeps lingering.

My sister Connie arrived, and we sat quietly alone with Jessica a good part of the day. I became the "scribe," since Jess was very vocal as she moved into a deeper phase of dying. Her voice had been weak all morning, but at 1 P.M. she cried out in a strong voice, "All right! All right! Come! One, two, three, OK, OK, here I come!" She also silently repeated the name of her husband, Ned, who died five years ago.

I felt privileged to record visits with her gardener and his little family, and with her neighbor, Faith Fuller. "I can't believe I'm going," she told Faith. "What communion we have here." To Raul she said, "God bless you. May we meet again in heaven. I have a tear in my eye." To his wife Maria and son Ivan she said, "I'll miss you," and "Beautiful people," as she kissed Maria's hand and Ivan's cheek, smiled and waved goodbye.

"Is everyone sleeping at our house?" she asked Connie, who answered, "Yes. Everyone's very close." "Good," said Jess, "I like that!" Then a long series of restless movements began, and every few minutes Jessica said, "How do I get out of here?" "How do I get out?" "I want to get out."

"Yes, you want to go home to God," soothed Jan. "I must go," insisted Jessica, "but I'm too weak." I responded, "Where you're going, you can go weak, and the weaker, the better." Jessica nodded and smiled at me beatifically. Then she pulled off the covers, tried to walk, and said, "I'm going to get dressed.

I guess I'm going around the corner. Let's go."

"Are you all right?" she asked Jan. "You look prettier and prettier." Jan responded, "Your heart's working so hard, it will give out soon and you can go to God." (Her heart is pumping 140 beats per minute and higher.) "Do you really feel that way?" Jessica asked longingly. "Will it be today?"

Day 7: January 8

Jessica is on a long journey, moving, but very slowly. It is taking a long time and getting harder for her. In whatever way I can, I am being a companion along the way, although I know that most of the way she must go alone.

"You can't take it with you," as we all know. This is writ large, sitting at Jessica's deathbed, surrounded by her books, family photographs, and lovely southwestern paintings. Perhaps this is why she keeps stripping off her sheets and her nightgown several times a day. Is she experiencing what Job did as he tore his gown and proclaimed: "Naked I came from my mother's womb, naked I shall return" (Job 1:21)? "She wants to get out of this body," said the hospice nurse. The literature reads: "The owner is no longer in need of a heavy, non-functioning vehicle."

After a peaceful morning sleeping, Jessica became very active and vocal around 2 P.M. For over an hour she repeatedly called out, "Take me! Home! Please. Take me to the end." At one point she shouted it loudly.

A dying person frequently makes restless repetitive motions, due partially to the decrease in oxygen to the brain and other metabolic changes. But the movements this afternoon seemed deliberate and directed. Jessica kept holding her arms out and strongly reaching forward, as though "someone" were there in front of her, which is probably the case. She also kept folding her hands in prayer, very unlike the aimless flailing motions.

To help calm and reorient her, I quietly told her that Connie and I were there, "watching" and praying with her. She gave us a big smile and almost laughed, then grabbed on to my hand as Connie rubbed her back to bring her some relief. It was hard to understand her, but she said, "I can't talk well. Hello, hello!"

She was extremely energetic for a dying person, and wanted us to sit her up, which we did with difficulty. Then on her own she rocked back and forth, trying to move. "I must be off," she announced clearly, as she pulled the sheets up over her head and groaned. Then she removed the sheet and stripped again. She put the nightgown over her head meticulously like a shawl and arranged her hair, saying, "I must go. Let's go."

She finally fell back to sleep again, exhausted. It felt as though she had completed some important phase. Jan, Connie and I sang Compline in Jessica's little oratory tonight instead of bedside.

Day 8: January 9

The Hospice guidelines explain that close to one or two days prior to death, the person may experience a surge of energy. "The spiritual energy for transition from this world to the next has arrived, and it is used for a time of physical expression before moving on." Was this what Jessica was doing yesterday?

Today a dramatic decline is evident. Jess seems farther away. Her eyes are closed constantly, and she doesn't talk. But throughout the day she moans and repeats "Uh-oh, uh-uh-uh-uh-uh-oh." She seems to be in great discomfort, especially in her legs. Rubbing and massaging only seems to help for short periods before she begins to groan again. It is a painful restless day for her, and an important opportunity for caregivers to let go and understand that there is only so much we can do to "fix" things.

The Hospice nurse came again. As we all gathered in the bedroom, she eloquently explained how Jessica is in the process of "active dying," doing it peacefully and well. I love the emphasis on *active* dying and on not interfering in the "mystery." The nurse also told us what to expect in the next seventy-two hours, which she guesses is the approximate time left. Then she demonstrated a technique called "healing touch" to help Jessica relax.

The nurse's wisdom and compassion were so enlightening and comforting. "You mean she won't be in agony, but we will?" asked Ted. "Yes," she said. Several of us wished we'd known all this earlier before Hospice was founded and we had to take care of dying parents without guidance or support.

Fr. Dave returned from Tucson and sat with Connie and me by Jessica's bedside to pray in silence. Jess did not seem aware of his presence, but when I told her he was there, she reached for him. He quietly read the scripture meditations from the Roman Catholic rituals for the dying, which seemed to calm Jessica and distract her from her discomfort. When he finished passages from the Gospel of John (14:1-6, 23, 27), Jessica said with difficulty, "Beautiful!" And when Connie and I concluded by singing "My soul is longing for your peace" again, she said, "I love that."

When we left for the evening, Jan insightfully said how glad she was that Jessica didn't die a week ago when Fr. Dave celebrated the Mass of the Transfiguration. Then we would have felt Jessica's absence too keenly, since she was still very much herself and very much with us. But now, as we watch her fade away more and more each day and struggle for release, the extra time helps us all let go of her more gradually and gladly, as we, too, long for her freedom.

Day 9: January 10

This morning I woke up at 4:30 and felt the weight of grief so heavy again, I sobbed and sobbed, then went to breakfast and ate an unhealthy white flour waffle for comfort food.

Jessica is a world. I have only to say her name, and the very sound of it, or the thought of her, conjures up that world. I know this will always be so, since there is really no death, only a change of worlds. (Did St. Paul say that, or Black Elk?) Because of my thirty-five years of spiritual connection with Jessica, as well as the intimacy of participating in the holiness of her dying, I expect to feel her presence beyond death more strongly than anyone else, even my mother. After all, Jessica will only be on the other side of "the door."

Yet at the same time, being Tessa of the Incarnation, an *embodied* spirit, I feel the loss of life-in-the-flesh more keenly each day as Jessica's flesh wastes away and I watch her drifting more and more into the heavenly realm, which is not a *place*, but a state of *being*. She will take her "body" with her and leave behind only her "corpse." The difference between body and corpse is a great mystery I do not comprehend.

I recall often hearing this gorgeous passage from Shakespeare: "Oh, that this too, too solid flesh would melt, thaw, and dissolve itself into a dew." It seemed so lofty and sublime before. But now, I watch Jessica's flesh melting away more and more each day. And each day the smell of death grows stronger as the "ketones" build up as a toxic waste product of cellular decomposition. Shakespeare's poetry does not feel so sublime now, and the ache in my heart grows larger.

Jessica chose a lovely Celtic cross to adorn her ashes. This afternoon, Loren, her son-in-law, glued it on to a "perfect" wooden box that had arrived for Christmas. It was beautiful to look through the window and watch him work so lovingly. It's good to have such touchstones of the end.

Jessica is clearly on "the other side" today. She doesn't speak and barely moves, with her eyes always closed. No more nightgown. She lies naked, covered only with a soft blue blanket. Her heart has slowed down, and her lungs are filling with fluid. It can't be long now.

Tomorrow is Jan's birthday. Jessica brought her into the world at 1:30 A.M. Jan hopes that her mother will die tomorrow so that from now on she'll celebrate two birthdays on January 11: hers into this world, Jessica's into the next world.

Day 10: January 11

Jessica was utterly gracious to the end and gave Jan the birthday gift she wanted. She died this morning at 3:45 A.M., simply, quietly, peacefully taking her last breath. The immediate family was gathered round the bed, holding hands, and bidding her farewell. Connie, Fr. Dave and I arrived after she expired, though we came as soon as Jan called. We sat together around the body with silent prayers and tears and individual memories of this great lady: mother, sister, friend to so many.

Wanda came from Hospice to declare Jessica officially dead. She said it was impossible to close Jess's mouth because of rigor mortis, but the jaw would relax and close soon. For now the eyes would not stay shut either, which is why our ancestors covered them with coins. As Connie said, "I always thought it was to pay Charon to row you across the river Styx!"

Jan and Ted dressed Jessica in an aqua nightgown. I added the blue blanket and a purple scarf. "What a sense of color!" said Ted. Jan put a crucifix in Jessica's hands, and Wanda helped remove her wedding and engagement rings. She noted that everyone was still whispering. "Yes," said Jan, "because this is very sacred space." More than one of us looked to see if Jessica would breathe again, although we knew she never would.

It was good to stay with the body, to kiss Jessica's hands and feet and forehead, to feel the flesh turn cold and waxen. Some people made phone calls, scrambled eggs and coffee, others sat and prayed Jessica along the final mysterious stage of her journey. I felt waves of grief and loss wash over me and collapsed on the bed next to hers and slept a little.

The Morning Star

Four hours later, we celebrated Mass around the body, which was one of Jessica's fondest desires. It's impossible to describe what it felt like because it was, as Loren said to me, "beautifully intense," "rapturously intense," "ecstatically intense." Fr. Dave blessed the body and all of us with holy water and a juniper branch from Jessica's trees. He blessed the box that will hold her ashes. So much of what he said was inspired in the moment, and with both the beauty and the grief, I can barely remember the words. Or the spontaneous "prayers of the faithful" we all made. I do recall that all the prayers were about gratitude and love and the sense that Jessica lives on in us, like Christ, as we continue to love one another and the whole world, with a heart as large as Jessica's, which left no one out.

We read John 14:1-6, 23, 27 once again for the Gospel. Connie and I sang Psalm 100. I felt such a mixture of gladness and grief. "Arise, come to your God, sing him your songs of rejoicing." When I got to the last verse, I choked on the words: "Go within his gates giving thanks, enter his courts with songs of praise," because I knew that Jessica had passed through those gates and into God's inner courtyard already. At the end of Mass Connie and I sang the chorus to "Morning Star" and many joined in to sing it again:

> *I have seen the morning star*
> *upon the distant horizon.*
> *All the shadows of the dark*
> *cannot keep the sun from rising.*

Out the bedroom window, I saw that the sun was indeed rising over the red rocks of Sedona and Jessica's rose garden. It was consoling to imagine how Jessica herself now shines like the sun over the whole world because she is no longer confined to time and space or the limitations of her body.

Then two men from the mortuary came to take Jessica's body away to be cremated. They did not wear black, and they did not drive a hearse. With utter sensitivity, they moved her body onto a stretcher, covered her with purple cloth, and then respectfully moved out of the way and invited us to say our last farewells. Connie and I led the body out to the vehicle with lighted candles to emphasize the ongoing sense of the sacred.

"This is the Morning"

Now I think of the last pages of the last book of the *Chronicles of Narnia*, by C.S. Lewis, when everyone has gone to heaven and learns that no good thing is ever destroyed. "The term is over: the holidays have begun. The dream is ended: this is the morning."

And then:

The things that began to happen after that were so great and beautiful that I cannot write them. And for us this is the end of all the stories, and we can most truly say that they all lived happily ever after. But for them it was only the beginning of the real story. All their life in this world and all their adventures in Narnia had only been the cover and the title page: now at last they were beginning Chapter One of the Great Story, which no one on earth has read: which goes on forever: in which every chapter is better than the one before.

35

Top Five Regrets of the Dying

What Would You Do Differently?

Tessa Bielecki

If you were to die today, what would you most regret? I do not find this a morbid question but a healthy self-examination with enormous ramifications for living fully in the present moment. Bronnie Ware, an Australian nurse who worked in palliative care for several years, recorded the dying "epiphanies" of her patients in the last three months of their lives. Her blog, "Inspiration and Chai," generated so much interest that she put her observations into a book entitled *The Top Five Regrets of the Dying*.

Common Themes

"When questioned about any regrets they had or anything they would do differently," Ware writes, "common themes surfaced again and again." As Susan Steiner wrote in *The Guardian*, "There was no mention of more sex or bungee jumps." Instead, these are the top five regrets of the dying.

1. I wish I'd had the courage to live a life true to myself, not the life others expected of me.
2. I wish I hadn't worked so hard.
3. I wish I'd had the courage to express my feelings.
4. I wish I had stayed in touch with my friends.
5. I wish that I had let myself be happier.

Unfulfilled Dreams

The first and most common regret has to do with our unfulfilled dreams. The second comes from every male patient Ware nursed. These men missed their children's youth and their partners' companionship. Yet all of us have the freedom to choose now to get off "the treadmill of a work existence."

By suppressing their feelings in the third top regret, people tried to keep peace with others and instead settled for a mediocre existence. They even developed illnesses relating to the bitterness and resentment they subsequently carried throughout their lives. Those who became too caught up in their own lives and let go of their "golden friendships" remembered the richness of old friends only when it was too late to track them down.

The last regret, not allowing ourselves to be happier, is perhaps surprising because we don't always recognize that happiness is a free human choice. Instead we remain enslaved by old patterns and thoughts. We pretend to others, and even worse, to ourselves, that we are content, when in truth we fear change and long to laugh harder and more often.

Steiner concludes her article by asking us the all-important question: "What is your greatest regret so far, and what will you set out to achieve or change before you die?"

36
Living Fully, Dying Well
Reflecting on Death to Find Your Life's Meaning
David Denny

Most of us try to avoid thinking about death—until the moment we come face to face with it. But when we have the courage to accept our inevitable mortality, and even to contemplate it actively, as a spiritual practice, we open the door to living fully, joyfully, and in complete presence. *Living Fully, Dying Well,* originally edited by Edward W. Bastian, Ph.D. and Tina L. Staley, LCSW, and then by Netanel Miles-Yépez, is an investigation into the challenge each of us faces: to embrace all of life from the beginning to the end.

Deathbed Revelations

When death approaches, many of us undergo a profound transformation—we let go of old distractions and focus with new clarity on what gives our life meaning. Yet we can invite these profound "deathbed revelations" at any point in our lives by engaging in an honest inquiry into our own mortality. *Living Fully, Dying Well* provides a doorway to begin your own exploration of the mysteries of death—from the cultural myths about dying, to the personal fears we all share, to the question of what becomes of us beyond this life.

Living Fully, Dying Well unfolds as a dialogue between spiritual leaders and medical healers: Rabbi Zalman Schachter-Shalomi, Joan Halifax Roshi, Dr. Ira Byock, Tessa Bielecki, and Marilyn M. Schlitz. Each of them brings a unique perspective to the universal human experience of death. These luminaries offer their stories, their insights, and their most valuable practices to transform death from a source of fear to an opportunity.

Part I is an interfaith dialogue between these leading spiritual teachers, scientists, and social workers concerning the spiritual, medical, scientific, and psychological aspects of dying, as well as their perspectives on the afterlife. Part II is an independent collection of resources: guided meditations, life-review practices, affirmations, and reflections.

The book illustrates how various perspectives on dying might enable us to live with more vitality and compassion, while also imparting wisdom to help our family, friends, and colleagues go on without us.

37

Remember to Live!

Embracing the Second Half of Life

Tessa Bielecki

Death is an inescapable part of the desert experience. In *Remember to Live,* Thomas Ryan guides us through the second half of life, which involves loss and grief, aging, illness, preparing for "a good death" and life after death, with radical implications for living fully now. He addresses these areas both poetically and practically and opens each chapter of his book with one of his own poems, quoting amply from other spiritual writers, including the Beatles. He enriches his work with testimonies from family, friends, and participants in his retreats on "Savoring Life by Facing our Mortality."

A Litany of Blessings

Every chapter concludes with suggestions for personal reflection, exercises, and discussion questions. I was charmed by his multiple numbered lists: five dynamics of aging, seven ritual elements for healthy grieving, ten ways to have more fun, five things God won't ask us on Judgment Day, four stages of forgiveness, six words to say to one another in order to die in peace or allow another to die peacefully.

A Personal Testament

Three outstanding exercises include looking at all your reasons to be grateful, then creating a litany of blessings; working through the Wheel of Life to find balance between key areas such as physical well-being, personal development and creativity, and spiritual attunement; and writing "A Testament" as though you only had a short time to live: What did you love most in life? What ideas brought you liberation? What sufferings seasoned you? Who is enshrined in your heart?

The second half of life becomes more peaceful when we plan ahead and take care of important documents: our will, power of attorney, and health care directives. It helps to write our own obituary and plan our funeral. Then we are free to age more creatively, to focus more on the inward than the outward journey, rereading our personal histories and sharing our stories. We may need to deal with unfinished business or downsize according to energy levels and needs, practicing letting go in little ways to be ready for the "big" letting go.

Fear of Dying

These topics are not morbid. Addressing them early in the second half of life helps us to live more vibrantly and consciously. We "sort out our priorities and realign the use of our time and energy and material resources to keep first things first.... We stop taking things for granted and putting things off for 'someday'."

Ryan's fine volume addresses our western discomfort with dying, distinguishes between sorrow and grief, stresses the importance of going to God the way God came to us: "in and through a body," and beautifully describes how "death and life touch each other at every moment of our existence... like lovers kissing." In the end, the author insists, "there's no getting around it: the best preparation for a good death is a good life. The work of dying well is, in large part, the work of living well."

38
My Desert Instinct

Facing Death and Loss

David Denny

I recently made a retreat at Desert House of Prayer, northwest of Tucson. It brought me back to my first retreats in Sedona, Arizona when I was twenty years old. This is partly because the Desert House was founded just after Fr. William McNamara began the Spiritual Life Institute in Sedona, and the older structures reminded me of some buildings at Nada, the name of SLI's retreat center, originally an old homestead.

The Wonder of Saguaro-land

Desert House's founder, Fr. John Kane, was aware of SLI's adventure, and the notebook in my cell refers to SLI's influence on Kane's vision. Silence, solitude and desert. But unlike Sedona, a chaparral landscape of red rock cliffs and buttes, Desert House is in the Sonoran Desert, surrounded by miles of saguaros and palo verdes, creosote, cholla and mesquite.

I let myself melt into the silence and simplicity, the dry emptiness, the sere, sheer wonder of saguaro-land. I roamed the library and checked out *The God Instinct* by Tom Stella and *The Secret Knowledge of Water* by Craig Childs. I didn't get far in either one because I slept a lot. But Stella's book brought me back to my earliest awakenings to the attraction of the contemplative life.

At the end of Mass Sunday morning, Fr. Tom Picton mentioned my presence and noted how Fr. McNamara had influenced Desert House. He also said that I used to edit *Desert Call*. So the retreat time was a beautiful, bittersweet immersion in a sense of continuity and legacy. After Mass, a woman approached and mentioned that she used to retreat often at Nada in Sedona.

I walked in an arroyo where I went many years ago with my father when I gave a retreat for him and some of his friends at Picture Rocks Retreat Center across the road from Desert House. It tugged at my heart to think how life has changed. The desert remains, and our sojourns are brief on earth. My parents were still alive, but my mother's Alzheimer's was advanced, and a month after my retreat, my father moved into assisted living.

The Ticking Clock

Mom had already moved into an Alzheimer's memory care residence. I will never forget the sound of her confused, pleading voice fading behind the glass door as it closed and locked behind Dad and me the first time we left her behind to inhabit her little room where Tessa had hung Mom's vibrant and colorful oil paintings.

One of the last times I saw her conscious, I sat and fed her as a parent feeds an infant. I don't know if she recognized me, but she looked grave, tried to speak, and the only word she uttered was "Beautiful."

It is difficult to live with the mystery that people we love mean the world to us, but they pass away while the world remains. It doesn't seem right that a man can die while his clothes remain behind. Is a clock grieved as it ticks away beyond the life of its owner? I think of the Gloria Fuertes poem that claims pens, doors, sheets, tables and chairs love us and miss us when we're gone: "What will come of things when we're gone? / They're like dogs that can't make it without their masters."

I recall a desperate cry of the heart in the face of death and loss. At the end of Shakespeare's *King Lear,* the dying king laments the loss of his daughter Cordelia and bellows, "Why should a dog, a horse, a rat have life, / And thou no breath at all? Thou'lt come no more, / Never, never, never, never, never."

Not many of us live in deserts, and we may be led to believe that a "desert experience" is foreign to dwellers in temperate zones of green meadows, wide rivers, and tall trees. But no one escapes Lear's "inner desert" of loss and "never."

Forever or Never Again?

One of St. Teresa of Avila's favorite words was "forever." Christianity is a hymn to "forever" and "eternity." But every Christian faces dark nights and must wrestle mightily with the fact of impermanence, Crucifixion and the "never again" of Jesus of Nazareth in flesh and blood. Can we make it without our Master?

Strange: despite my grief and loss, I come away from this desert retreat, as always, with a sense of gratitude and renewed awe at the desert's beauty and the nourishment I derive from its silent nights, cool dawns and dusks of low sun and long shadows, skittering lizards and wailing coyotes.

Postscript: The Edge Effect
David Denny

Desert Voices is an attempt to write, even sing, from the edge, the frontier, the ecotone. It celebrates the amorous border between two "desert rats" and an arid landscape of sand, sky, and giant cactus. It celebrates friendships between Abrahamic brothers and sisters who have spent too much time demonizing each other. It mourns the lives lost along the border of Israel and Palestine and honors non-violent sowers of hope. And it sings from the death bed, from the poverty of the Cross, the universal desert of impermanence that may be the shadow of eternal life.

Ecotones

I was nineteen when I learned about "ecotones" from ornithologist Dr. Amadeo Rea, who taught ecology at Prescott College. Even at that young age, I had already experienced the notion, not as a biological phenomenon, but as cultural and religious experience. I spent my seventeenth summer as an exchange student in Afghanistan and my twentieth birthday in a Buddhist retreat center. Both adventures were disturbing and wondrous. They took me to "edges," to encounters with the unknown. My childhood frames of reference shattered.

But a new intuition dawned, a hunger and a taste for the vitality I found in these unsettling frontiers, a wonder at the possibility of a "frameless" God in whom everyone lives and moves and has being, and in whom our lives and cultures and spiritualities blossom through encounters with the "other," the "alien," who turns out to be human, and to know, feel, understand aspects of life unknown to me and uncharted on my little globe, my American-European Christian map of the world.

In these years, the nineteen sixties and seventies, I also saw the mirror image of the ecotone: race riots, political assassinations, and that indelible magazine photo of a naked Vietnamese girl fleeing her napalm-burned village, her terror-stricken face streaming with tears. I was haunted: what is the face of America for Afghans? The face of American Christians for Vietnamese? The face of Christianity for Jews or Muslims?

A New Edge

Now we have arrived in the twenty-first century, and it is autumn for Tessa and me. We have only recently begun the Desert Foundation and remain full of creative energy. But we are at a new "edge," a change of seasons, as we approach the last years of our lives. We have more to harvest, but we have offered here some "first fruits" from our little garden on the fecund edge. The violent tragedies with which we grew up, and the hope and hunger for a transformation in Christ, for a wisdom that may go deeper than the political and religious thought and practice that led to bloodshed, drove us to the desert. We believe something beautiful and nourishing has bloomed there, and we hope you have found some nourishment in these pages.

As I sit in my living room, I admire a painting my mother created when she was about the age I am now, the painting you see on the cover of *Desert Voices* and here in black and white. It depicts the Sonoran Desert with which my mother, too, fell in love. It is sunset. The desert sky includes some thin gunmetal grey clouds but is mostly aglow with red, orange, and yellow on the horizon above the chalky blue mountains of the Santa Rita range east of our home in Green Valley, Arizona. In the foreground, stones reflect the glowing sky in their subdued, grave, stony way. In the near distance, three elongated saguaros rise out of a patch of darkness, silhouetted against mountain and sky. It is the radiant edge of day and night, mountain and desert, earth and sky.

A Love Letter

I also think of the painting as a love letter from my mother. She was not a big talker or writer. And in the final years of her living with Alzheimer's disease, she didn't even know she had sent this "letter." She is gone now, but her dark patch, her glowing sunset, and the tall, thin saguaros between them suggest to me that there is more to earth, love, and our lives than time.

Her message means that sunset here is sunrise elsewhere, that there is another side to her glowing painting and her mortal life. The dark desert patch may be a seedbed, a womb. Divinity has become flesh and stone, and all of us on this little planet are sticking together forever in love.

So let's go to the edge of our territory, bury the hatchet, erect a tent, plant some corn in the desert, listen to each other's voices, sleep under the stars, and wait for sunrise.

About the Authors

Tessa Bielecki and Fr. David Denny have worked together for almost forty-five years. They began as Carmelite monks at the Spiritual Life Institute in the desert of Sedona, Arizona, where they co-edited *Desert Call* and gave retreats and workshops. At Colorado College they taught *Fire and Light: A History of Christian Mysticism* and *Desert Spirituality: from the Middle East to the American Southwest.*

They left monastic life in 2005 and created the Desert Foundation (see www.sandandsky.org) and now live in neighboring hermitages near Crestone, Colorado, in the spirit of the Christian Mothers and Fathers of the desert.

Tessa recorded *Wild at Heart: Radical Teachings of the Christian Mystics* for Sounds True, and is the author of three books on St. Teresa of Avila, most recently *Holy Daring.*

Fr. Dave has served as chaplain for *Image* journal's Glen Workshops and Seattle Pacific University's writing residencies. He raises funds for Cross Catholic Outreach, a relief and development ministry for the poorest of the poor.

Both authors are currently working on their memoirs. They co-authored *Season of Glad Songs: A Christmas Anthology,* and continue to teach on Christian mysticism, desert spirituality, and the contemplative life at retreats and workshops around the world.

Notes

Introduction: Desert Harvest

i Desert Foundation saguaro logo by David Denny

Part One: Desert Love Affair

1 © iStock.com/SRabin

18 Hogan photo by Tessa Bielecki

20 Tessa Bielecki photo by David Denny

22 James Foy, who died in 2014, was a physician, writer, and professor of psychiatry at Georgetown University School of Medicine. His poetry is published in medical journals, literary magazines, and an anthology, *Blood and Bone: Poems by Physicians*. He was a good friend of the Desert Foundation and especially supported our life as contemporary hermits. Dr. Foy selected this icon of Saints Anthony and Paul.

31 Photo of Ned and Jessica Danson by Tessa Bielecki

Part Two: The Tent of Meeting

41 © Can Stock Photo Inc./SandyS

42 Photo of al-Hadiyah hermitage by David Denny

44 You can help struggling Palestinians by ordering their crafts from www.sunbula.org.

47 Photo of Tessa Bielecki and Reb Zalman Schachter by Netanel Miles-Yépez

49 Reprinted from *Presence: An International Journal of Spiritual Direction,* 19.3, page 61 (Spiritual Directors International ©2013) and used with permission

51 Reprinted from *Presence: An International Journal of Spiritual Direction*, 18.2, page 61 (Spiritual Directors International © 2012) and used with permission

53 Jo L'Abbate lives in Florida and teaches English as a second language to Arabic-speaking students.

58 To learn more about Dar al-Islam and their annual Teachers Institute in Abiquiu, New Mexico, visit daralislam.org.

70 To order *Three Faiths, One God*, visit www.threefaithsonegod.com.

Part Three: Walls and Bridges

115 Photo of the Holy Sepulcher by Tessa Bielecki

121 Photo of Tessa Bielecki and David Denny at the Wall by Joy Lapp, who led our fact-finding pilgrimage to Israel/Palestine

122 You may purchase *Holy Land: Common Ground* from the director at Edward.Gaffney@valpo.edu.

127 Photo of Tessa Bielecki and David Denny with Amal Elsana Alh'jooj by Joy Lapp

128 The Circles of Change event is sponsored by Building Bridges, a non-profit organization whose Building Bridges MEUS program brings together young women, ages sixteen-nineteen, from Israel, Palestine and the United States to participate in intensive summer programs that include training in communication and leadership in order to help create more just, inclusive societies.

130 Painting by Netanel Miles-Yépez and henna design by Moriah Ferrús

134 Photo of "Women in Black" by David Denny. Tessa Bielecki stands on the right, with Joan Fairweather from Ottawa in the middle, and Iris Keltz from

Albuquerque on the left. Their signs in Hebrew and Arabic say "End the Occupation."

137 If you are interested in making a similar "fact-finding trip" to Israel/Palestine, visit http://www.sabeelcolorado. org/?q=fact-finding-trips or contact lappj@earthlink. net.

138 Reprinted by permission from the January 29, 2008 issue of the *Christian Century*

141 © STRINGER/Reuters/Corbis

Part Four: The Inner Desert

145 © Can Stock Photo Inc./gitanna

164 Reprinted from *Presence: An International Journal of Spiritual Direction*, 18.4, page 62 (Spiritual Directors International © 2012) and used with permission

166 Saguaro photo by Tessa Bielecki

169 Art by Marilyn L. Denny

Acknowledgements

We are grateful to Dennis Brown, Kristen Kauffman, Laura Keim, Netanel Miles-Yépez, Paul Baynham, and Pegge Erkeneff, who encourage our vocations as contemplatives and writers and also support us by serving on the Desert Foundation Board of Directors. Netanel urged us to "harvest" our writings and suggested we create Sand and Sky Publishing.

We are also grateful to Gary and Joanne Boyce and the Nicholas and Pansy Schenck Foundation. When we became homeless after 2005, they built hermitages for us adjacent to their cattle ranch, silent and solitary spaces where we write, pray, and live out our lives as contemplatives and writers.